christmas
inspirations

rose hammick
charlotte packer

christmas
inspirations

Practical ideas for creating beautiful gifts
and decorations for the holiday season

RYLAND
PETERS
& SMALL

LONDON NEW YORK

photography by jo tyler

Senior designer Catherine Griffin
Senior editor Annabel Morgan
Location research Claire Hector
Production manager Patricia Harrington
Art director Gabriella Le Grazie
Publishing director Alison Starling

Stylist Rose Hammick
Text Charlotte Packer
Recipes Clementine Young

First published in the United States in 2004 by
Ryland Peters & Small, Inc.
519 Broadway
5th Floor
New York, NY 10012
www.rylandpeters.com

10 9 8 7 6 5 4 3 2 1

Text, design, and photographs
© Ryland Peters & Small, Inc. 2004

Library of Congress Cataloging-in-Publication Data

Hammick, Rose.
  Christmas inspirations : practical ideas for creating
beautiful gifts and decorations for the holiday
season / Rose Hammick, Charlotte Packer ;
photography by Jo Tyler.
      p. cm.
  Includes index.
  ISBN 1-84172-683-4
  1. Christmas decorations. 2. Interior decoration. I.
Packer, Charlotte.
  II. Title.
  NK2115.5.C45H35 2004
  747'.93--dc22
                              2004005702

Printed and bound in China.

contents

introduction

At Christmastime our homes take center stage, as we invite friends and family to celebrate with us. Everyone has their own particular favorite aspect of Christmas; the tradition they look forward to most keenly—decorating the tree, or baking the Christmas cookies (for children it must certainly be hanging out their Christmas stockings!)—and without this element, Christmas just wouldn't be Christmas. Whether you see it as a time for gathering with family and friends to indulge in some well-loved annual traditions, or whether your approach is more spiritual, Christmas is a celebration that happily manages to be all things to all people. It's a magical time: long, dark nights and homes filled with the aroma of mulled wine, eggnog, and other delicious treats.

We can all list the key ingredients of a traditional Christmas, but every family observes them in its own way. It might appear to be a rather unchanging festival, but a glance through the family photo album will show that Christmas is a celebration that is constantly evolving. Whatever happened to that artificial silver tree that took pride of place in 1972, or the plastic nativity set you loved so much as a child but have conveniently erased from memory?

Part of the fun of Christmas is the way in which we dress up our homes for the season each year. *Christmas Inspirations* is a collection of imaginative ideas and decorative schemes that will hopefully encourage you to indulge in this aspect of the festival, to update your Christmas celebrations and perhaps even create a few new traditions of your own.

OPPOSITE: Christmas decorations can come in many guises; here a crocheted key ring looks charming nestling in the tree.
OPPOSITE INSET: A tartan bow is all it takes to get family pets into the spirit of the season.
ABOVE RIGHT: Hyacinths make a change from evergreen foliage such as holly and ivy, and they scent the house beautifully, too.
RIGHT: A jaunty bow and pipe-cleaner antlers transform a draft-excluder sausage dog into a festive-looking reindeer.

styles and inspirations

Whether your style tends towards the relaxed and informal or is better described as contemporary and chic, the following pages explore four very different schemes that can easily be adapted to suit your own home and your family's celebrations.

Every family has its own unique Christmas rituals: gifts from Santa Claus left in stockings or pillowcases; presents before or after lunch; eggnog spiked or alcohol-free; midnight mass on Christmas Eve or church on Christmas day. But despite this, the idea of a Traditional Christmas lives on.

traditional style

The look of the traditional Christmas as we know it is something we have to thank the Victorians for. In December 1848, an engraving depicting Queen Victoria and Prince Albert in front of a Christmas tree appeared in *The Illustrated London News*. The tree was decorated with gilt gingerbread and on each tier there were at least 12 candles. This opulent tree, not to mention the presents piled beneath it, has set the tone ever since.

Even the colors we traditionally associate with Christmas—the rich reds, dark forest greens, and bold plaids—come to us straight from the Victorians. They are also the colors of winter berries and foliage, but the typical Victorian dining room and drawing room had dark red or green walls and were lit by the warm glow of gaslights or candles.

In America and the UK there remains a real affection for Victoriana, and Christmas is the obvious time for families to indulge in a little nostalgia. This is why the heavily decorated tree and elaborate table settings remain such popular elements: these rich, formal decorations lend our homes a Victorian or Edwardian ambience regardless of when they were built.

ABOVE LEFT: Silk flowers and delicate birds fashioned from feathers make charming tree decorations.
ABOVE CENTER AND RIGHT: Antique flatware and vintage linen strike just the right note if you want your table to look as traditional as possible at Christmas. Parcel tags tied to knives and forks with pretty ribbon make novel name cards.
OPPOSITE: A Grand Fir, with its open branches, is the perfect foil for these antique and reproduction decorations. Lengths of wide ribbon make a pretty alternative to gaudy tinsel.

RIGHT: A towering display of frosted fruits recalls the opulence of the Victorian dining table, as do the silver candelabras. Don't feel you need to play safe with the colour of your candles; here, deep purple looks wonderful against the ink-blue walls.
OPPOSITE BELOW LEFT: A napkin is secured with sea holly and a pink-tipped rose in place of a napkin ring.
OPPOSITE BELOW RIGHT: A fat tartan bow adds a festive finish to a stack of damask napkins on the sideboard.
OPPOSITE ABOVE RIGHT: These richly coloured bead blackberries look stunning with the purple candles.

Decorating on a grand scale also offers a welcome change from ordinary day-to-day living and entertaining—few of us tend to have the time or money to indulge in full-on floral arrangements, and rarely when we entertain do we run to lavish table settings replete with candles, flowers, and towers of frosted fruit. But at Christmastime it's somehow more acceptable to indulge ourselves, and to treat our families and friends to a visual feast in keeping with the traditional turkey and all its trimmings.

This style of Christmas decoration is really self-explanatory. As its name suggests, Traditional Style is all about warmth, security, and nostalgia, and as a look, it's easy to adapt to any style of home. Rich colors can work brilliantly within contemporary interiors, and an elegant Grand Fir decorated with glittering baubles and tiny tin toys would look really dramatic in a minimally furnished all-white interior—a little unexpected maybe, but there's nothing wrong with a few surprises at this time of year.

The traditional look can be taken as far as you wish or toned down and given a vintage, shabby-chic spin. But, whatever your approach, take care that the quest for authenticity doesn't result in your home looking like a store display window. If a color scheme based on reds and greens seems too ordinary, you could replace them with rich jewel colors such as purples, deep berry pinks, and inky blues to lend the look a more contemporary edge.

For mantelpiece, door, and table decorations, large boughs of holly and viburnum or trailing strands of ivy are the obvious choices. Pairing foliage with jewel-bright anemones, richly colored roses, and soft silvery-purple thistle heads will result in a table setting that remains rooted in tradition but still looks fresh, individual, and elegant.

Formality is really the key to the traditional-style Christmas table, and a tablecloth, sparkling glassware, and fine china are all essential. A white tablecloth is the foundation for a traditional Christmas table, and if you scout around antiques markets you may be lucky enough to stumble across a heavy linen or damask cloth and some sets of napkins to match. If you don't have a tablecloth, a cotton sheet with a runner placed along the center will do the trick, and you could customize either the napkins or napkin rings to match. Plain white china is extremely versatile and can be dressed up with bold plates placed beneath it and a colored tablecloth and napkins. If you have any decorative china hiding away in cupboards, this is the time of year to get it out and show it off.

Good glassware is easy to come by as most department stores have a range of affordable designs, many of them based on classic Victorian and Georgian styles. Alternatively, use everyday tumblers and accessorize with wine glasses in vibrant jewel colors such as purple, red, or blue.

RIGHT AND FAR RIGHT: Frosted fruit looks magical and is an easy way to create an impressive centerpiece. Brush the fruit with egg white then dust with sugar. Use a skewer to hold the fruit to avoid finger marks in the frosting. Let dry overnight before arranging on a stand. Here the fruit has been displayed on four old glass cake stands, stacked one on top of another.

RIGHT: A centerpiece of purple thistle heads, sea holly, snowberries, and pink-tipped roses makes a refreshing change from more conventional holly and ivy-based Christmas arrangements. The bouquet also complements the muted tones of the tartan runner on the table.

THIS PAGE AND OPPOSITE ABOVE LEFT:
A central arrangement of bare twigs and glossy red berries is decorated with wooden angels, stars, and hearts.
OPPOSITE ABOVE RIGHT: *In Scandinavia, decorating the tree involves using simple, often homemade decorations such as woven straw hearts and umbrellas, and delicious gingerbread cookies that are tied onto the tree with bright red ribbon.*
OPPOSITE BELOW: *Some families have sets of Christmas tableware, which come out every December. Napkins and tablecloths are usually white with red embroidery.*

Tranquil and understated, Scandinavian interiors have a timeless elegance that gives them a universal appeal. And never more so than at Christmas when homes are lit by candlelight and filled with sweetly scented flowers and simple red and white decorations.

nordic style

Christmas Nordic-style is refreshingly un-glitzy—the perfect antidote to the increasing commercialization of the festival. The emphasis is on bringing a sense of light and warmth into the home at a time in the year when the days are short and spring seems a long way off. The appearance of candles in windows is a magical and uplifting sight. Upper windows are often decorated with stars and a braided corn wreath is tied to the front door.

Because of their simplicity, Christmas decorations tend to appear all over the home in Scandinavia, rather than being confined to public areas like the hall and sitting room. Handmade decorations and large bowls of deliciously scented hyacinths and striking amaryllis are displayed throughout the house, on landings and in guest rooms. Many families have special sets of Christmas table linen that have been handed down through the generations and which are brought out every year. Some people even go so far as to change their normal curtains for more Christmassy red and white ones.

gingerbread is a favorite Christmas decoration—trees are hung with gingerbread hearts, angels, and stars

Perhaps the nicest thing about many Nordic-style decorations is that they can be made at home with the family. Garlands of nuts, cut-out paper stars and snowflakes, and little clothespeg fairies and Santa Clauses can easily be assembled during a happy afternoon with scissors and glue at the kitchen table. Gingerbread, in particular, is a favorite means of decoration, and in Scandinavian countries, trees are often hung with gingerbread hearts, angels, and stars. Virtually every household has an intricately decorated gingerbread house on display.

And, just as the decorations are easy to make, the basics, such as china and tablecloths, are not hard to assemble either. A plain white tablecloth can be left as it is or given a more Scandi spin with the addition of a cheerful red-and-white gingham runner or, if you are feeling creative, decorated with a bold appliquéd border of red holly leaves or simple stars. Use cookie cutters as stencils and cut the shapes from felt or scraps of red-and-white fabric. They can then be sewn or fabric-glued around the edges of the cloth. Napkins can be decorated in the same way. At the heart of a Nordic Christmas is the sense of homespun charm, so making your own tablecloth and napkins or customizing cheap store-bought ones is perfectly in keeping with the way in which Christmas is celebrated in Scandinavia.

OPPOSITE LEFT: Gingerbread houses are popular edible decorations and are even available in flat-pack kits. For a gingerbread recipe, see page 117.
LEFT: Flowers, such as scented white hyacinths and these elegant amaryllis stems, are an important part of the Scandinavian Christmas and provide a welcome taste of spring at the darkest point of the year. Buy stems in bloom, tie them with ribbon, and anchor them in a chunk of floral foam, then cover it with silver moss.
ABOVE: Most homes will have some form of simple candelabra, such as this plain iron design.

OPPOSITE AND FAR LEFT: A circle of straw dolls is a really traditional Nordic decoration, and the sort of thing that will have been passed down from generation to generation.
I FFT: Scandinavian homes are filled with candlelight throughout December, and candles are placed in windows to cheer passers-by. In recent years, simple wooden stands featuring animals and nativity scenes with electric "candles" have become popular and are widely available. For suppliers, see page 124.
BELOW: Dishes of candies and nuts serve as decorations in their own right. Here, a name tag has been added to a dainty dish of candies in place of a name card at the dinner table.

When it comes to setting the table, you may well find that you've got most of the essential elements already. If you don't have one, a set of serviceable white china and some plain, good-quality glassware is a worthwhile investment as it's so versatile. Candles are another essential—again, the plainer the better. These days even supermarkets stock thick church candles in the run up to Christmas, and honey-scented beeswax candles, tiny votives, and elegant tapers are also widely available.

In terms of adaptability, the Scandinavian look is a cinch. Because the colors and shapes are so strong and simple, they can be worked into almost all but the most eclectic interiors, and even then, with a little judicious editing of ornaments and soft furnishings, it can be done.

Christmas Nordic-style demonstrates that less is more—a real Christmas tree, piney and aromatic, decked out with simple homemade decorations and surrounded by scented white flowers, red berries, and the warm glow of candlelight will look nothing short of magical.

Layering white on white is a lovely way to bring a little winter magic into the home at Christmas. It's also the perfect decorative solution for the contemporary interior, in which a traditional scheme might look incongruous.

contemporary whites

ABOVE: Fir branches, sprayed white with florists' spray, provide an informal base for a contemporary arrangement of taper candles and iridescent glass baubles.
RIGHT: A bare-branched fir tree is the perfect choice for keen recyclers as well as minimalists in search of an alternative to the standard spruce—

here, a fir tree has been stripped of its needles and sprayed white before having its lower branches bulked out with frosted twigs.
OPPOSITE ABOVE RIGHT: Delicate snowflakes cut from white tissue paper and stuck to the window with spray adhesive are easy to make (see page 94) and look stunning.

The concept of a chic contemporary Christmas may seem something of a contradiction in terms, but even the best-loved traditions can benefit from the occasional update. If you've always found the inevitable preparations for Christmas more of a chore than a pleasure, then abandoning its conventional trappings in favor of something lighter, brighter, and more contemporary might be just what you need to get into the spirit of the season.

Freshening up Christmas and giving it a modern spin doesn't mean you have to abandon the much-loved tree or stint on the Christmas decorations. A more contemporary celebration just requires a little lateral thinking, and the most obvious way to bring Christmas right up to date is to adopt one main color for your decorative theme.

White, the minimalist's favorite, is the ideal color for the job. Clean and modern but also soft, dreamy, and perfectly in keeping with a winter festival, thanks to its connotations of ice and snow, white is a flattering foil and works well in virtually any interior, from a spacious open-plan loft space to a more conventional family home.

THIS PAGE: This all-white table setting combines a sense of occasion with a sense of fun. There's a slightly kitsch Winter Wonderland overtone, but the simple china and the limited color palette make it sophisticated, too. To make a similar frosted forest, arrange whitened twigs (available from most florists) in damp floral foam, then conceal the foam beneath a cloud of white feathers (in this case, an old feather boa).
OPPOSITE LEFT: A garlanded present set on every plate makes a pleasant and decorative surprise for your guests.
OPPOSITE RIGHT: Group candles in metal troughs amid iridescent baubles.

Texture and variety of tone are the key to the success of a one-color theme. Think of white in its broadest sense, so that your palette includes silver and pewter as well as various rich shades of cream. You can also add touches of gold here and there as long as you go for old gold rather than shiny new gilt. The overall mood you are aiming for is contemporary elegance. Look for decorations with unusual finishes—pearlescent or feathered baubles, for example, and add accessories in galvanized metal, translucent porcelain, and delicate hand-blown glass.

For a truly contemporary scheme keep the decorations relatively minimal—a flurry of delicate tissue-paper snowflakes dotted around a large expanse of window looks very effective, while a garland of tiny Christmas tree lights suspended from a mantelpiece is a nod to the traditional floral swag. Instead of a traditional Christmas tree, attach a trail of lights to a wall in the outline of a tree. To inject a little

co-ordinate the **clean lines** of a contemporary home with sensational **sparkle** and **fluffy** feathers

LEFT AND BELOW LEFT:
Candlelight adds warmth and
character to any interior, and
this is especially important
when the interior is entirely
white. These candles were
made with colored wax from
a candle kit poured into
hollowed-out gourds, and
surrounded by simple wreaths
made from sprigs of holly, fir, and
viburnum. They bring a subtle
splash of color and textural
interest to an all-white scheme.

kitsch into the proceedings, buy a bright white artificial tree
and accessorize it with a family of white flock polar bears as
a secular alternative to the nativity scene.

Although a totally white theme means that you could
avoid greenery altogether, if you do want to include some,
keep the flowers light and avoid too much dark, heavy
foliage. White roses are always pretty, while bowls of white
hyacinths and amaryllis are easy to come by in the winter
and will also scent the house deliciously.

It's worth remembering that the strongest decorative
statements are often the simplest. A large bowl filled with a
mixture of baubles in shades of white and silver will look
stunning on a hall table or heaped in an open fireplace. Soft,
flickering candlelight is the best way to add warmth to a
cool minimalist interior. Buy candles in different shapes and
sizes such as fat church candles, delicate tapers, and tiny
votives, and group them around the house.

Even if you're usually drawn to richly colored Christmas
decorations, you'll find that a limited palette can be just as
festive. White decorations with flashes of silver and gold,
combined with lots of twinkling tiny lights, will look just as
Christmassy as their more traditional counterparts.

LEFT: A shower of tiny twinkling white "icicle" lights not only provides a more minimal alternative to the traditional swag, but also enlivens an empty fireplace.
ABOVE: Don't limit your use of baubles and other decorations to the tree. Here, sparkly little beaded silver stars intended to hang on the tree make a magical display along the mantelpiece when interspersed with tiny votive candles.

contemporary whites 27

Hot pinks and vivid blues may not be the colors that leap to mind when thinking about Christmas, but they're ideal if you're tired of more traditional decorations. Used with skill, vibrant colors can make Christmas stylish and funky as well as festive.

contemporary brights

ABOVE: Although made with real pastry, these little mincemeat pies were designed to be used as festive candleholders. When massed together and the pretty pastel candles are lit, they make a charming and unexpected table decoration.
ABOVE RIGHT: Bold and bright, these glorious striped baubles are the perfect tree decoration for a more colorful and contemporary Christmas scheme.

Once you've decided to abandon traditional Christmas colors, you'll find that there is no limit to what you can do. However, there are a few rules to bear in mind—after all, allowing yourself a free rein with bright, bold color doesn't mean that taste and style should take a back seat.

The key to using lots of color is to think in terms of tone (strong or muted, saturated or pastel), then to choose just one or two and stick to them. Dark colors look wonderfully dramatic when paired with contrasting, acid shades as they act as a foil for one another, and when more muted shades are used together, the overall effect is subtle and sophisticated. But pair colors at random and with no clear emphasis, and your scheme will look decidedly off-key. For a retro 1950s feel, stick to decorations in sugary pastel shades; while for a look with a little more oomph, take a package of sugar-coated candies as your inspiration and go wild with hot, juicy colors instead.

The other important thing to remember is to restrict your use of pattern and keep it bold rather than fussy—go for bold stripes and spots, for instance, as you want the look to be strong and modern, not cutesy and contrived. Bright, striped, multicolored baubles will look fabulous bobbing alongside plain ones; add anything else and the impact will be diminished.

THIS PAGE: Not all trees need be store-bought. A sculptural alternative to the traditional tree can be made by bending lengths of armature wire into two rough tree outlines, which are then fixed together at right angles. All the "tree" needs in the way of decoration is a collection of multicolored baubles suspended on lengths of fine wire or bright ribbon.

OPPOSITE AND LEFT: A funky multicolored Plexiglass hanging mobile in juicy fruit shades is given a festive makeover with the addition of a blizzard of homemade tissue-paper snowflakes (see page 94 for details of how to make them) and Christmas trees.

ABOVE: A heavenly host of homemade clothespeg angels adds festive color to the staircase. These angels would also look good hung in front of windows, as well as on the tree. They are easy to make—simply glue scraps of felt and fabric around wooden clothespegs, which are available from traditional hardware stores.

contemporary brights 31

Bright tree decorations have the advantage of looking good whatever style of tree you choose, traditional or alternative. For the presents stacked at the bottom of the tree, use wrapping paper featuring the same bold geometric designs as on the decorations above—stripes or polka dots—or better still opt for the simplicity of plain, bright tissue paper and finish off the gifts with flamboyant ribbons in contrasting colors.

Christmas stockings look wonderful in bright fabrics, and when suspended from the fireplace they can become a central part of a contemporary bold and bright decorative scheme. A string of multicolored lights wound among the stockings can create a wonderfully kitsch grotto effect that your children will adore. But don't feel you have to limit your Christmas lights to the small twinkling variety. There are now many different styles of Christmas light to choose from, including sophisticated Oriental-style mini-lanterns, and all are stunning strung along shelves and across ceilings. These lights look particularly good in the kitchen, a room that is often overlooked when the Christmas decorations go up.

Colorful Christmas flowers are easily adapted to any scheme. Forget about the usual Christmas greenery, and opt for something exotic instead. Visit your local florist and see what's in stock, before selecting something that will work best with the colors you've chosen for your decorations, regardless of whether or not the flowers feel Christmassy.

When it comes to the Christmas table, you can make the look as formal or relaxed as you want. If you have a set of plates in jazzy colors, these will be perfect: you could even mix and match using different colors, though this effect only really works if the plates are all the same style and not patterned. If your china is white, splash out on wine glasses the color of lollipops, or give the table a lift with bright cotton napkins and a matching runner.

Once you've decided to opt for a bright and funky Christmas, you'll find it easy to adapt to whatever style of home you have, and both you and your guests will benefit from a dose of zingy carnival color, especially if you are celebrating Christmas in a wintry location!

OPPOSITE AND ABOVE: These days Christmas tree lights come in a vast array of designs, and although it's tempting to stick with the charm and simplicity of the traditional white variety, something quirkier can be just as magical. These Oriental-looking lights are made from brightly colored handmade paper stretched across twisted wire frames and embellished with sequins and glitter. They look so beautiful it would be tempting to keep them up all year round.

The anticipation and excitement that we remember from childhood Christmases is recaptured the very moment the first decorations go up. Suddenly our homes are transformed: dressed up with lights, ribbons, baubles, and flowers, all ready for the party season. The decorations you have may be old or new, but the pleasure they give is as powerful as ever.

deck the halls

The Christmas tree is the absolute epitome of Christmas for many families, and a celebration without one would be inconceivable. Christmas lunch may vary, and sadly the stocking eventually stops arriving, but there will always be a Christmas tree. And decorating it is the highlight of the preparations.

decorating the tree

Surprisingly, the tree as a symbol of Christmas is a fairly recent development. For many centuries, trees played no part in our Christmas celebrations at all. The custom of bringing fir trees into the house at Christmas is thought to have originated in Northern Europe, probably in Germany. The tradition traveled to America along with German settlers, and first arrived in England with Queen Charlotte, wife of George III, although it was actually Prince Albert, Queen Victoria's German husband, who popularized the custom. Since its arrival, the tree has remained central to the Christmas festival, as important to those for whom Christmas is a religious and spiritual celebration as it is for those who enjoy it on a purely secular level. Either way, it's not until the tree arrives in our homes that Christmas really begins.

Trends in trees may come and go and the real versus fake debate will rumble on, but many people agree that nothing beats a big, freshly cut Christmas tree. It is a magical thing and its distinctive resiny smell alone gives the house a Christmassy air in an instant.

From the beginning of December, stalls selling Christmas trees spring up on street corners everywhere Christmas is celebrated. But, if you have one nearby, try contacting your local forestry services instead, and find out when their trees go on sale. You will no doubt get a better tree at a better price, and some forestry services

RIGHT: When buying decorations, don't limit yourself to the most obvious Christmas themes, such as Santa Clauses, snowmen, and angels. These delicate, glitter-tipped butterflies and pearlescent shells look absolutely magical hidden among the branches, especially when the Christmas lights are twinkling.

LEFT: Rather than opting for a bright white artificial
tree, why not coat a real tree with florist's spray to
create the effect of a delicate frosting of snow?
Alternatively, white car paint will give a thicker, more
opaque coating. Because of paint fumes, the spraying
should be done outside and the tree left to dry for
an hour or so before you begin the decorating.
ABOVE: A glass ball, as light as a soap bubble,
perfectly complements the delicate paper butterflies.

decorating the tree 37

ABOVE: The traditional Victorian tree was an opulent affair. Here, rich red and purple glass balls, chandelier drops, lavish imitation flowers and tiny feathered birds, lavender hearts and silk slippers recreate the mood.
ABOVE RIGHT: Real candles are the nicest way to light the tree, but once lit, must not be left unattended. They are available from candle shops and Christmas stores.
BELOW: Search out decorations with an antique feel.

will even allow you to choose your tree and then cut it for you. This is also the best way to find specific varieties, such as the elegant open-branched Grand Fir or the bushier Nordic Spruce.

Despite their beauty, many people find the prospect of dealing with a real tree (and all those needles) something of a chore. Luckily, the days when artificial trees were regarded as unacceptably tacky are far behind us. Not only are there many incredibly realistic artificial trees available nowadays, there are also lots of delicious scented oils that you can use to make up for the artificial tree's telltale lack of smell.

The completely unashamedly fake white tree—once upon a time the ultimate display of bad taste—is also enjoying a renaissance, becoming a bold statement of cool chic or irony, depending on how kitsch or restrained the decorations may be. And finally, there are now lots of wonderful alternative trees, ranging from sculptural twists of curly hazel twigs to "trees" made from slices of flat-pack Plexiglass or wall-mounted fiber optic strands.

THIS PAGE: Birds of all kinds were hugely popular tree decorations in the 19th century, and were made from tin and glass as well as real feathers. Although it's possible to find original designs at antique fairs and through dealers, they are becoming more and more expensive. Luckily, excellent copies such as this bird with real feathers are widely available. Bead berries and satin ribbon are more subtle alternatives to contemporary decorations such as tinsel.

LEFT: With its mix of homemade and store-bought decorations, this generous-sized tree looks fresh and pretty, and is complemented by a pile of presents that have been wrapped in understated brown paper and tied with simple red ribbons.

BELOW: A shallow bowl of aromatic cinnamon bundles looks every bit as good as it smells, and is a great alternative to pot pourri. Don't buy the expensive high-quality cinnamon sticks used for cooking. Instead, look in florists for packs of the lower-grade cinnamon sticks that are intended for use in flower arranging. The smell is every bit as good, but they are much cheaper.

BOTTOM: A crocheted teddy keyring doubles up as both decoration and present—perfect if you're hosting a children's Christmas party.

RIGHT: Striking and elegant, these simple origami paper stars are cheap and easy to make, and look lovely against the reflective silver baubles.

Dressing the tree should be exciting, but before getting started, it's worth thinking about the overall effect you are hoping to achieve. Your choice of tree—real or fake, traditional or modern—will be based on the style of your home and the way in which you and your family celebrate Christmas. For some families, decorating the Christmas tree is nothing short of a ritual—the box containing decorations that are used year after year is ceremoniously brought down from the attic, and everyone adorns the tree while sipping the first mulled wine of the season. For others, each year's tree provides an excuse to splash out on new decorations and go for a totally fresh look. Instead of the box in the attic, it's a case of delving into shopping bags filled with exciting goodies you've just hauled home from some fancy stores.

Either way, getting the decorations right is absolutely key. Even a majestic seven-foot Nordic Spruce will look disappointing when festooned in cheap tinsel and hung with dingy decorations that have seen better days. Conversely, a large display of hazel twigs may sound minimal (or even bleak) to some, but when decked out with a selection of carefully chosen baubles and other decorations, it can look sensational.

ABOVE: White twigs added to the tree at strategic points create the impression of a light frosting of snow. The tree is decorated Nordic-style with corn umbrellas, gingerbread shapes, and simple baubles.

RIGHT: This Shaker-style tree is laden with clothespeg fairies, homemade gingerbread (see recipe on page 117), and decorations made from natural materials. The striped ribbon brings all the colors together.

LEFT: Baked cookie stars can double up as delicious Christmas tree decorations when made with glowing jam centers that catch the light.

ABOVE: For a Nordic-style tree, look out for designs with naive, homemade charm, such as this resin snowflake, which looks as though it has been crocheted.

mix beautiful baubles with homemade decorations for a truly wonderful effect

ABOVE: A cascade of brightly striped and acid-colored baubles hover around the bold silhouette of this bent wire tree (for instructions on making the tree, see page 29). Some are suspended from nylon thread to create the impression they are floating.
OPPOSITE: This bare-branched tree is the perfect choice if you are keen on recycling. Saved from the previous year for its graphic beauty, the tree has been filled out with wintry white twigs to create more bulk and to improve its shape. It is decorated with fragile cut-paper snowflakes and small translucent baubles (see page 94 for details on how to make the snowflakes).

Whatever your approach, take the time to consider how you intend to decorate the rest of your home. The tree must tie in with other decorations and displays. If you're planning to fill the house with greenery—trailing lengths of ivy, sprigs of holly, and fiery red poinsettias—then a Grand Fir adorned with delicate feather birds, tin toys, and glossy glass balls in reds and greens will be perfect. So, too, would a Shaker-inspired tree adorned with simple hearts and stars. If your tastes are more contemporary, a traditional tree will look incongruous, so opt for galvanized metal buckets containing dramatic displays of wintry white twigs or a bold sculptural arrangement of metal armature wire twisted into the shape of a tree (see left), which would be much more fitting.

As well as considering your decor, bear in mind the amount of entertaining you are planning. If you have small children, then a tree laden with simple wooden decorations is perfect—fun to decorate together and not too showy. But if you are hosting a cocktail party, a little more glamor is in order—bright bows and baubles and twinkling lights. If you're planning a Christmas cookie swap, you could decorate the tree with edible treats, such as gingerbread hearts and stars. Similarly, if one of your children has a Christmas birthday, the tree can double up as a giant goodie bag, its branches laden with candies and going-home presents. If your Christmas will be child-free, on the other hand, you can indulge in exquisite and fragile decorations—look for delicate and unusual pieces in white, silver, and gold, such as lustrous shells, birds, and feather butterflies, and mix them up with chandelier-style glass-crystal beads.

And, finally, just as important as the decorations, think about exactly where you want to place your tree for maximum impact—once fully decorated and trailing Christmas lights, it will be hard to move. Placing a tree in front of a window is lovely—the twinkling lights will be reflected in the glass of the window and your home will look wonderfully festive and inviting from outside.

OPPOSITE: A wood-burning stove surrounded by a decoratively stacked log-pile looks suitably wintry and needs only a few decorative touches such as the leylandii branches draping the mantel and oversized glass balls.
RIGHT AND FAR RIGHT: The hallway, often overlooked when it comes to Christmas decorations, can be made wonderfully festive and welcoming with the addition of winter foliage wound around the stair bannisters and studded with pretty baubles.
BELOW RIGHT: A chunky garland of peanuts with a decorative ribbon is understated yet festive.

There is nothing more welcoming than a wreath on the front door at Christmas. The fact that our doors remain largely unadorned throughout the rest of the year, save the odd cluster of bright balloons for a child's birthday, makes the sudden appearance of wreathes of holly or glossy red berries a cheering sight, redolent of Christmas.

wreaths and garlands

Simple ready-made wreaths and garlands are widely available and can be customized to create a more personal statement. Select a wreath that is a suitable scale for your door—something too small will look cutesy and contrived, while a wreath that is too big will look ridiculous, no matter how beautiful the flowers and foliage. Consider the color of your front door and choose foliage that either complements it or provides a strong contrast.

Once you've thought about the scale and the colors that will work best, take a look in your own garden and see what you can forage. Many city gardens have an abundance of ivy; a staple ingredient in both garlands and wreaths, and larger gardens may have at least one or two good-sized evergreen shrubs with attractive foliage. If you live in the country, extend your search to nearby lanes and woodland. Branches of holly, bay, viburnum, and skimmia will

THIS PAGE AND RIGHT: A traditional wreath of holly, viburnum, and snowberries is studded with deep red roses for added luxury. Although a bright red bow is the obvious choice for a wreath like this, the russet ribbon used here is more subtle and ensures that the arrangement is extremely elegant.

OPPOSITE RIGHT: The dark foliage of viburnum, holly, and bay is enlivened with the bright poppy-like anemones. The glossy red holly berries and the smaller more subtle viburnum berries provide more color as well as texture, and the ribbon, which secures it to the door, is a final, dramatic touch.

all add structure and bulk to arrangements. Look for interesting leaf forms and unusual colors such as *Berberis thunbergii*, which has attractive small purple leaves.

Berries are also an essential part of any Christmas wreath or garland and cotoneaster, a common garden shrub, has them in abundance, in glossy red, orange, or yellow, depending on the variety. Plump white snowberries (*Symphoricarpos albus*) are also a common sight in winter, as are the slightly surreal-looking purple berries of *Callicarpa bodinieri*. And last, but by no means least, there is mistletoe—although you will have to pay a visit to a local market or florist to get your hands on some. Get as much mistletoe as you can—a generous bunch in the hallway looks particularly festive and will inspire much more enthusiastic kissing than a single sprig!

Grasses such as miscanthus and pampas are back in vogue, and their pale, feathery flower heads look magical in a wreath.

Honesty seedheads (*Lunaria*) often look so beautiful in the winter sun that you may feel reluctant to cut them down, but a wreath of these alone will look wonderfully ethereal.

If you don't have your own garden, all these plants are available from good florists. And a visit to the florist is always worthwhile, because this is where you'll find all those additional flowers that will transform your arrangement into something out of the ordinary. Roses, in the strong jewel colors that contrast with dark foliage, work particularly well, as they are both festive and luxurious.

Although it is customary to have a "living" wreath created with flowers, foliage, and berries, wreaths fashioned from bare, twisted twigs are also widely available—sculptural and suitably wintry, they can make a welcome change from the usual greenery. Many stores stock a range of such designs, as well as more intricate arrangements crafted from wire threaded with glass beads, which look like frosted branches.

Don't feel you have to limit your use of wreaths to the front door alone. Small wreaths shaped in circles or hearts look pretty hung from the backs of chairs. Larger wreaths hung at the top of mirrors make dramatic and elegant focal points.

OPPOSITE PAGE: Not all garlands must be green. Here, beaded wire, feather butterflies, and glass baubles are used in place of winter foliage.
THIS PAGE FAR LEFT: An imposing globe concocted from a selection of winter twigs and foliage has been sprayed white with car paint for a more dramatic statement.
LEFT AND ABOVE: A delicate wire wreath, decorated with tiny heart-shaped beads, looks charming casually hooked on a cupboard door.

LEFT: A tightly packed heart-shaped twig wreath is tied to a chair with pretty ribbon.

ABOVE: Dried citrus fruits are as seasonal in a wreath as they are in a cake.

OPPOSITE: A large shaggy wreath of dried pink peppercorns is unusual and dramatic and complements this soft grey door better than darker, heavier foliage. Pink peppercorns are available from flower markets and specialty outlets, but their season is short, so ask a florist to order them for you if necessary.

ABOVE: Once you've put up the tree and tackled the main rooms in the house, decorating the guest room may seem like a chore. A simple paper garland hung along the headboard is the perfect solution—quick, easy, and festive.

OPPOSITE BELOW RIGHT: This wreath is incredibly simple—stark, even—and looks stunning hung in the hallway from a Shaker peg rail. Perfect if you want to extend your decorations beyond the living room, but prefer to keep them understated.

Little beaded wreaths hung from hooks on a dresser or perhaps a door handle will bring unexpected festive touches to every corner of the house.

The mantelpiece is the traditional place for garlands, but they can look spectacular elsewhere. Trails of greenery intertwined with baubles, ribbons, and twinkling lights then wound around the bannisters will give any hallway a Christmassy makeover. Some houses have ceiling beams, which look fantastic dressed up with garlands and swags.

As with wreaths, garlands don't necessarily have to involve real greenery. The paperchain is the obvious example, and is still central to a child's Christmas experience. You and your children can experiment and create other kinds of cut-paper garlands, such as simple rows of stars and hearts, or winged angels and crowned kings. Look for alternatives in the stores such as decorative strings of tiny woolen mittens or jolly Santa Clauses, or make your own, suspending clothespeg fairies from a length of twine or cord. A length of ribbon to which baubles, stars, and other tree decorations have been attached can form a magical decoration when hung from the ceiling in a child's bedroom. And a simple but immediately effective way to decorate a guest bedroom is to hang a garland of silk hearts filled with lavender above the bed.

the mantelpiece
is the traditional place for heavy garlands but they
look spectacular elsewhere

ABOVE: Here the headboard in a spare bedroom has been decorated with a more luxurious, though less overtly Christmassy, garland of silk hearts and slippers. The lavender-scented hearts should encourage a good night's sleep and the beading on both slippers and hearts provides a pretty decorative touch. This is the sort of decoration that you could choose to leave up all year round, and it could be embellished with a few baubles come December.

wreaths and garlands 55

OPPOSITE: Think laterally about displaying cards. A toast rack is the ideal holder for cards that were too late for other arrangements.
RIGHT: A miniature clothes line, with scaled down, glitter-coated clothes-pegs, is both a witty and convenient way to display your cards.
BELOW: A length of twig mesh, available from most florists, becomes an ideal temporary 'pin board' for Christmas cards.

As the Christmas cards start to arrive, finding space for them can be a problem. The answer is to regard them as Christmas decorations in their own right. Cards relegated to the top of the television, or a dusty shelf will never look anything other than forlorn.

displaying cards

When deciding where to display Christmas cards, it's worth remembering that they look best en masse rather than dotted around the room. The best solution is to clear a side table or shelf and dedicate it to your cards, taking some care with their arrangement—the largest stacked at the back and the smallest in front—obvious, really, but easily overlooked. Cards prone to slipping and doing the splits can be secured with adhesive gum or tape.

One of the easiest ways to arrange a mass display of cards is on shelves filled with books. Slide the backs of the cards between the volumes and the Christmas images are then suspended across the spines of the books. There is something pleasingly casual about this approach, as there is with tucking smaller cards around a mirror frame. For a look that's more considered, suspend cards on lengths of ribbon weighted with baubles or crystal drops. Cards on ribbons also look pretty suspended in windows. Remember the backs will be on show as well, so cover them with bright paper in different colors—then the windows look as good from the outside as they do within.

your christmas cards will look more effective en masse than when dotted all around the room

Empty stretches of wall can be enlivened with panels of fabric hung at regular intervals onto which cards can be pinned as they arrive. This also prevents causing any permanent damage to wallpaper or paintwork. Twig mesh, which is available in long lengths from florists, is particularly good for this sort of random group display; just punch a hole in each card and tie it onto the mesh with bright ribbon, raffia, or yarn.

If you don't want cards in your living room, or you run out of space, display them in the hallway. Lengths of ribbon or strips of fabric tied to the bannisters look great when glimpsed from other rooms and will brighten up an area that is often overlooked when it comes to Christmas decorations.

Your children may receive cards of their own, and could use them to make a mobile for their rooms. Just sandwich lengths of tinsel between two cards and glue around the edges, then hang the tinsel at different heights from two sticks arranged as a cross and decorated with paint, tinsel, or ribbon.

ABOVE LEFT: For an understated but effective way to display Christmas cards, simply open them and slip the back in between two books. For a more festive finish, you can add ribbons and baubles too.
OPPOSITE AND ABOVE: The hall stairs are the perfect place from which to display a selection of Christmas cards. Take different lengths of medium-width ribbon and weight one end with a glass bauble or chandelier crystal, then attach the cards by sandwiching them around the ribbon and sealing the edges with a little glue. Finally, tie the ribbon to the bottom of the bannisters or secure the ends under the stair carpet.

LEFT AND BELOW RIGHT: A pretty arrangement of scented candles surrounded by red berries and winter foliage is a welcoming sight in the hall. Glossy red baubles (chosen to echo the berries above) are tied to the drawer handles with hot orange ribbon, which reflects the oriental character of the chest of drawers and also adds an extra festive flourish.
RIGHT AND FAR RIGHT: Make a large batch of spicy Christmas potpourri and pile it in the deepest bowls you can find for a dramatic and richly scented table decoration. Choose the ingredients on the basis of appearance as well as aroma.

For most families, decorating the tree and the living room and making the dining-room table look beautiful on Christmas day is decoration enough. But extending your decorations to include the rest of the house is well worth the extra effort, especially if you are throwing a Christmas party or have invited friends or family to stay for the holidays.

decorative displays

The hall is the obvious place for additional decorative displays—it's where we welcome guests, and it's an area where people often congregate during big parties. It's not necessary to assemble anything particularly lavish or ornate—just a few simple touches to create the right atmosphere. A cluster of chunky church candles of varying heights surrounded by foliage and berries, and set in a large shallow dish on a hall table is enough to create a warm and welcoming atmosphere. Hang a big bunch of mistletoe close to the front door and deck pictures and mirrors with swags of greenery.

Smaller bowls of seasonal nuts, fruits, and wrapped candies not only look pretty but are useful to have on hand, as this is the time of year when you may find yourself hosting an impromptu gathering. Similarly, pots of strongly scented winter-flowering bulbs, such as cyclamen and hyacinths, placed around the house—on landings, on windowsills, and even in the bathroom— will give your home an air of being all dressed up for visitors.

ABOVE: The mantelpiece in a child's bedroom is the perfect place for a Christmas display, especially if the child is either too young to really understand Christmas, or older and less inclined to go for the total tinsel option. Antique decorations are supplemented with a row of colorful glass balls hung from pretty ribbons.

LEFT: These simple white ceramic tree decorations make a dramatic statement suspended against a dark fireplace.

RIGHT: A collection of hand-carved and hand-painted wooden animals are arranged alongside silver tree decorations and lit with candles to create a magical shimmering display.

OPPOSITE: A child's toys have been given a simple seasonal makeover with the addition of judiciously placed festive bows.

The kitchen is often overlooked when it comes to Christmas decorations yet, when there is a party, this room seems to be a magnet for guests. As with the hallway, it's best to keep any arrangements simple and unfussy—lots of ornate adornment isn't compatible with a kitchen's more functional role. Something as simple as suspending colored baubles from the hooks on a dresser looks pretty and also adds to the sense of occasion.

In many homes nowadays the kitchen is an open-plan space that also serves as a dining room and, if there are children, a playroom, too. You can make a virtue of this by extending your table decorations, in a pared-down form, to the cooking area—a few twinkling lights strung along shelves, or perhaps a big vase of sculptural twigs hung with glossy red berries. Give any larger toys (such as a rocking horse, dollhouse, or fort) that cannot be put away a Christmassy twist with a few bows and baubles.

Fresh flowers are always a good way to spruce up the spare room in readiness for guests. At Christmas it's nice to take this a little further. Take your cue from the living room and use a few decorations similar to those on the Christmas

ABOVE: A garland of tiny woolen mittens is a fun alternative to paperchains and tinsel and works particularly well with an understated, homespun decorative theme.

tree to create a small garland for the mantelpiece, to tie to the handle of the closet, or hang above the mirror. Aromatically scented candles surrounded by circlets of evergreen foliage look pretty on dressing tables and bedside tables, as do tiny votives arranged along a shelf, the mantelpiece, or even the windowsill. You could even make organza Christmas stockings filled with spicy potpourri, as a richly scented seasonal alternative to lavender pillows and small dishes of traditional potpourri.

Older children may want to decorate their own rooms, but younger children and babies will obviously need help. An unused fireplace can be hung with twinkling lights or clothespeg angels, while simple paper stars and snowflakes can be transformed into a Christmas mobile to entrance small children who are only beginning to understand what Christmas is all about.

Don't forget your own bedroom in all of this either. The mantelpiece, if you have one, is the obvious place for a decorative display—scented candles mixed with a selection of decorations is all that you'll need to remind you first thing in the morning and last thing at night, that Christmas is on its way.

THIS PAGE AND OPPOSITE ABOVE AND BELOW RIGHT:
Dainty little Christmas lavender bags can be used as
decorations as well as to scent the room. Here they adorn a
wooden dove on a side cupboard and are complemented with
hanging baubles and a handmade Christmas stocking.

decorate
each and every corner of the **house** leaving no doorway, window, or stair untouched for a truly **festive** look

OPPOSITE: Don't limit your use of potpourri to little bowls dotted around the house. These organza Christmas stockings contain a home-made batch of potpourri scented with a mix of essential oils, blended to create a suitably spicy Christmas aroma. To make similar stockings, just cut organza into stocking shapes, sew together, and fill with potpourri.

LEFT: These store-bought wooden stars look pretty scattered among the bags and scarves on the back of the door, and smell good, too, having been customized with a few drops of various Christmassy essential oils.

Sitting down to a delicious meal with close friends and family is one of life's greatest pleasures. This is especially true at Christmas, when the main meal, whether eaten at midday or in the evening, is central to the celebration.

table settings

When you consider the time and energy, not to mention money, that we spend on this annual feast, it makes sense that we should also take a little care over the appearance of the table. A table that has been thoughtfully arranged adds an extra dimension of enjoyment to the meal.

To make the effort worthwhile, it's best to opt for a decorative setting that is versatile enough to last for several meals over the holiday period. This way, the table decorations will earn their keep, and you'll also prolong a sense of festivity. Not everything has to be used for every meal—the look can be built up with each successive meal, starting on Christmas Eve. Laying the table with a tablecloth and matching napkins for a simple candlelit supper, even if it is just bread and soup, will get the festivities off on the right note. Then for Christmas lunch or dinner, the addition of a decorative runner, candles, napkins, place cards, and a more elaborate centerpiece, will transform the table and create a sense of occasion.

OPPOSITE FAR LEFT: A traditional centerpiece of winter foliage—holly and viburnum—is given a more contemporary feel with the addition of bright anemones and some glossy tree balls. LEFT AND DETAIL OPPOSITE RIGHT: The muted plaid runner with a brighter trim gives this table setting a traditional feel. The plaid ribbon and anemone flowers are a pretty alternative to napkin rings, and the candles in the center are surrounded by an unusual combination of ornamental cabbages and more anemones. ABOVE: Woolly handmade sheep make unusual party favors and look appealing emerging from their place-card shelters.

Some families have a special dinner service they bring out for Christmas every year. If this has a distinctive pattern or color, obviously it should set the tone for the rest of the table decorations. A table set with deep, bold colors and luscious foliage would look odd with daintily patterned blue and white china, however pretty. But those same blue and white plates, paired with loosely massed white hyacinths and a blue cloth, can look very festive, and the addition of candles in matching colors will make it Christmassy, too.

If you don't have a special set of china, your Christmas meal need not be any less festive. Think about what you have and use it as as your starting point, also bearing in mind the decorations elsewhere in the house. Obviously, the plainer your china, the greater its versatility. Simple white plates have the advantage over patterned, as they will work well whether the look you opt for is Victorian opulence or minimalist chic.

ABOVE: Give place cards an angelic touch—adorn them with silver wings or singing angels cut from sheets of craft metal. Attach your designs to fine wire threaded through the folded card so that they bob delicately above each name.
RIGHT: Match napkin rings to a table setting by using sprigs of foliage and left-over flowers or berries tied together with garden twine
OPPOSITE: The Christmas table should be a feast for all the senses, and cardamom pears not only look beautiful but scent the room, too. Take a chunk of floral foam, available from florists, and carve into a pear shape. Stick a twig into the top and stud with cardamom pods secured with glue.
OPPOSITE (INSET): Simple tumblers are perfect containers for charming party favors. The delicate white cheesecloth twists contain silvered chocolates and sugared almonds.

LEFT: A fresh, springlike centerpiece of scented hyacinths, twigs, and berries is perfect for a Nordic-style Christmas table.
ABOVE: Sprigs of bare white twigs and clustered scarlet berries look wonderful against these red napkins.
OPPOSITE: Although the chubby church candle, dark foliage, and rich red roses and berries are essentially traditional, this arrangement is given a more contemporary edge with the addition of a handful of sculptural white twigs.

When it comes to flowers for the table, think beyond the usual wreath of holly surrounding a cluster of candles and consider something more relaxed, even spring-like, such as cut flowers. Snowberries, dark pink hydrangeas, roses, and viburnum, for example, can make a centerpiece that is both fresh and festive. For something entirely different, use a row of tiny potted cyclamen to form a low hedge along the middle of the table, or arrange long trails of ivy around tiny votive candles. Napkin rings contrived from lengths of evergreen foliage will complement the table flowers perfectly.

If you are having a large family gathering with lots of children, a children's table is an excellent way to keep stress (and noise) levels down. Under-fives find it hard to sit still at the best of times, and at Christmas it's virtually impossible.

red and gold
always create fantastic Christmas themes for the table and around the house

LEFT: Make fun place cards for a children's dinner table by sewing initialed felt stars onto card stock.
RIGHT: British Christmas crackers can be depended on to start the festivites with a bang. These ones were made using a kit. Stack them in a pile at the bottom of the tree or put one at each place.
BELOW: Younger guests will be completely seduced by a plastic tree decorated with brightly wrapped candies and yummy lollipops!

While adults enjoy a long, leisurely Christmas meal, under-fives would often rather not eat at all, unless the meal being offered is based entirely around candies! A separate table makes the Christmas meal fun for small children and more relaxed for their parents. If you have several teenagers, they will also enjoy a table of their own, no doubt appreciating the privacy it brings. If you don't have a spare table, a low coffee table surrounded by oversized cushions would do—and be more fun and informal, too.

Place cards are the final detail you need to consider. Most department stores sell simple silver-plated or metal stands into which you can slip name cards, but not many people entertain in a fashion that makes them a worthwhile investment, and it is easy to make your own place cards instead. A plain buff parcel tag tied to a napkin with ribbon and flowers is understated yet chic. Once you start thinking about them, the options are endless—add name tags to Christmas crackers and party favors, or tie name tags to individual wreaths hung from the backs of chairs. It's these tiny details that will make it clear that this is not just a smarter-than-usual Sunday dinner, but a special celebration.

THIS PAGE: If younger members of the family will be seated at a separate table on Christmas day, you can have lots of fun devising a table setting based around primary colors and a fabulous fake tree studded with brightly colored candies. Plain paper cups contain bright napkins and wax crayons, so that the children can decorate the white paper tablecloth and even their plain white plates.

Intimate and mellow, candlelight is an essential part of any celebration. This is especially true at Christmastime, when simply lighting a cluster of pretty votives in glass holders creates a festive feel and a warm and magical atmosphere.

candles

BELOW: Choose richly colored candles to complement the foliage or berries that you place around them.

RIGHT: Making an ordinary candle look like a solid beeswax one is easy. Warm a sheet of beeswax on a radiator or over a flame, then wrap around your candle and secure at the back with a pin.

FAR RIGHT: Think beyond traditional combinations like holly and ivy. Instead, take inspiration from what's available at your local florist. Here, floating candles create tiny points of light dancing betweeen miniature ornamental cabbages and bright anemones.

Many of us use candles on a regular basis, either to scent our homes or to create a more relaxing atmosphere, but it's important to make sure that the candles used at Christmas are a little more festive than usual. They don't have to be particularly expensive, but if they're scented with Christmas spices, then so much the better.

The traditional place for candles at Christmas is, of course, on the tree. But although a candlelit tree looks breathtakingly romantic and beautiful, you will need to watch it like a hawk, and certainly never leave it unattended, even for a second. If you're determined to have candles on your tree, there are a few rules. You will need proper candleholders designed expressly for use on Christmas trees, and when you attach the candles to the tree you must take care not to place them under overhanging branches or too near other decorations. Keeping the tree from drying out is another important precaution—sit the base of the tree in a bucket of water and keep it topped up throughout the Christmas period. However, it's a lot easier and less high-maintenance to restrict your use of candles to tables, mantelpieces, and windowsills.

Candles make wonderful decorations in their own right and these days they're available in virtually any shape, size, or color and can be selected to match whatever decorative theme you may have chosen.

When choosing candles for the table, try to think beyond the traditional white or cream and consider a color that matches your flowers or ties in with the décor of the room. White and cream candles are elegant and timeless but darker colored candles are more dramatic and unusual.

Placing candles in the window is a Nordic tradition, and you can buy Swedish-style wooden candle stands from stores specializing in traditional decorations. The same effect can be created by arranging votives, either in pretty glass holders or paper bags cut with snowflake motifs, along a windowsill. Candles placed in front of mirrors look especially magical, as their twinkling light is intensified by the mirror and bounced back into the room. If you don't have an over-mantel mirror, place a cluster of votives on a silver tray or mirrored surface for a similar effect.

candles should be used to create atmosphere— they are essential at Christmastime

ABOVE: A church candle in a hurricane lamp is given added interest with a garland of dried hydrangea heads.
RIGHT: Gold crowns are not just a cute addition to these votive holders—they also disguise the fact that the holders are simply recycled babyfood jars.
FAR RIGHT: Paper bags with snowflake cut-outs are available from specialty candle shops. Alternatively, you can make your own from store-bought lunchbags. For safety, never leave them unattended.

Making your own candles is relatively easy, though it needs care since it involves working with hot wax, and is not something to do with young children. There are craft stores and mail order catalogs that specialize in candle-making equipment, and all you need to worry about is the style of candle you wish to make. Pouring wax into pretty mother-of-pearl shells is a nice alternative to votives, while hollowing out a winter gourd provides a good mold for making a chunky candle to use at the center of a floral arrangement.

Customizing store-bought candles is easier than making them from scratch, and something your children can do, too. Sheets of beeswax (available from craft stores) look good wrapped around plain church candles. And plain white candles can be given a Christmas makeover with holly leaves and snowflakes painted on their sides using poster paints.

OPPOSITE: Old flowerpots filled with berries and foliage are a good alternative to traditional candlesticks and are well suited to the look of old-fashioned beeswax candles.
LEFT: Arranging candles en masse always provides more impact. Here, pretty pink-and-silver mirrored candle holders are grouped together on a pierced metal tray.
ABOVE: An antique wall sconce is given a Christmas update with a funky bauble, a matching candle, and a pretty ribbon.

LEFT AND BELOW RIGHT: An Advent tree is a lovely way to decorate a child's playroom. Either look for a small open-branched tree, or lop the top off a really large tree. It's important that the tree is not too dense, so that the numbered gifts are not only visible, but also easy to remove when the day arrives.

The Advent calendar is not only the first decoration to appear in most households, it's also the one that best expresses the sense of anticipation and excitement of the season: as your children open the windows, they know that Christmas is on its way at last.

advent calendars

The tradition of the Advent calendar dates back to the 19th century, when it was common practice among devout families to mark the days until Christmas Eve. Some simply chalked lines on their front doors to mark each day of Advent as it passed, while others lit candles, either a single candle marked with 24 notches, or an arrangement of four candles, each one representing a Sunday of Advent.

It wasn't until the mid-1800s that Advent calendars as we know them now began to be produced, but by the turn of the century they had become lavish affairs. These days, however, it's getting harder to track down attractive designs that aren't merely chocolate-filled marketing tools for the latest cartoon characters. Yes, of course, your children will love them, but they are not remotely festive, and are usually anything but stylish.

Surprising your children with an unexpected alternative is a much nicer and more exciting way for them to enter into the spirit of the season. A miniature Christmas tree decked with 24 numbered mittens or socks, each one containing a little treat—chocolate coins, or perhaps tiny decorations

LEFT AND BELOW: *If buying a tree for your children's Advent count-down seems excessive, create your own "tree" using bare twigs. Take your kids to the park and collect them together, or buy them from a local florist. Arrange the twigs in a sand-filled container, like a galvanized metal bucket, then decorate the branches with numbered presents tied on with ribbon. Here, tiny baby socks were decorated with multicolored felt spots before being numbered, filled with presents, and tied at random to the branches.*

they can then add to the tree—will be far more novel than any store-bought offering. In a similar vein, you could suspend 24 numbered packages or miniature buckets from lengths of ribbon or a swag of Christmas greenery. Older children and adults might enjoy 24 Advent envelopes pegged to a clothes line, each one containing a silly riddle or puzzle, or perhaps a question to a quiz which can be marked on Christmas Day.

If you prefer the traditional windowed-style Advent calendar, it's not too difficult to make one for your children or to help them design calendars for one another. Choose a simple image, such as the front of your house, and get them to paint it or draw it onto card stock. You could even take a digital photograph, print it out on a large piece of paper and spray-mount that onto card stock. Next, cut 24 little flaps, and number each one. On a separate piece of card stock, mark where the flaps will open and fill each space with an image—magazines and family photographs are a good source of surprise elements. Before sticking the two pieces of card stock together, bend the flaps back into place so they don't open earlier than they are supposed to!

use your own home as inspiration for this year's homemade Advent calendar

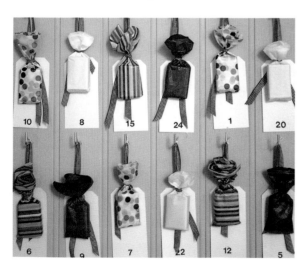

ABOVE LEFT: A hand-painted calendar will always be so much more personal than anything available in the stores, especially if the images inside each window relate to your family.
LEFT: As so often in life, the simplest solutions are the best. Here, bright wrapping paper and ribbon transform a panel of numbered hooks into an enticing countdown to Christmas.

OPPOSITE: A line of tiny galvanized buckets is a fun and imaginative way to count the days until Christmas. Available at little cost from markets, the buckets are a worthwhile investment as this hanging Advent calendar will no doubt become a family tradition. Each bucket is lined with a pretty scrap of fabric, which is not merely decorative, but also serves to conceal its contents.

The Christmas stocking must surely top every child's "best-bit-of-Christmas" list. And, if parents are honest, the stocking is probably the present they have the most fun putting together. For younger children, waking up to a laden Christmas stocking is particularly thrilling, because of course they really do believe that Santa Claus has delivered the presents in person!

christmas stockings

The tradition of the Christmas stocking is important because its roots are also those of Santa Claus himself. Around A.D. 270, St. Nicholas, the bishop of Myra, in what is now Turkey, made secret donations to the poor by slipping into their houses at night and leaving coins in their shoes and socks for them to find the following morning. His generosity led to his being sanctified, and of course, St. Nicholas, alternatively known as Father Christmas, is our very own Santa Claus, which is why we leave stockings out on Christmas Eve.

Although hanging up old socks remains popular, the stores are now filled with sumptuously decorated versions. Making your own decorative stocking is not difficult if you are handy with a needle and thread: draw a template on card stock or newspaper, and use this to cut out shapes from pieces of fabric. Stitch two pieces together, right sides in, and then turn the stocking inside out. Additional decoration can be appliqued, embroidered, or glued on.

LEFT AND OPPOSITE: Funky colored corduroy stockings with fake-fur cuffs are a jolly addition to the mantelpiece, both before and after Santa Claus has paid a visit. To make something similar, draw a large sock shape onto a piece of card stock to create a template and then cut out your fabric. Sew together, inside out, on a sewing machine and then either sew or glue the fur into place.

BELOW: A line-up of real socks in varying shapes and sizes have been pressed into service for Christmas Eve, and because they are all pure wool in muted retro colors, they make a stylish, understated display. Perhaps the partner to each sock could be wrapped up and popped in among the other presents, so that the pair of socks itself becomes one of the presents.

Personalizing the stockings with names or initials ensures that there will be no fights over who gets what on Christmas day. Making a patchwork stocking is more time-consuming, but the end result is worth it, and it will no doubt become a family heirloom, passed down through the generations.

Although stockings are considered more traditional, in many families pillowcases or small sacks are the order of the day. Sacks couldn't be easier to make, and plain burlap is available in all department stores, though an old sheet will do just as well. You can either line it with pretty fabric or sew a ribbon border to the top for a decorative effect.

If you have guests staying for Christmas, a miniature version of the Christmas sack would make a nice treat. You could make pretty felt bags containing one or two little gifts to be placed on bedside tables or outside bedroom doors. This will ensure that no one feels left out on Christmas morning, and it will also be a treat for anyone too grown up to get a visit from Santa Claus. As well as being cheap to buy, felt comes in a wide range of fabulous colors and it's very easy to work with.

And finally, which stocking tradition suits you best? British tradition has you waking up on Christmas morning to the delicious weight and lovely crinkly sound of a stocking lying heavy across your legs. American tradition has you trundling sleepy-eyed into the living room, to find your stocking no longer hanging from the mantel, but on the floor in front of the fireplace, brimming with goodies and gifts. Either way, make sure your children leave a drink for Santa Claus and a few carrots for his reindeer, and then watch their faces as they race in the next morning to see not only bulging stockings, but also nibbled carrot tops and an empty glass!

ABOVE: These angels are not just pretty decorations, but miniature "stockings" too. They have each been fashioned from scraps of bright fabric, and embellished with beaded trim. Their bodies, which open at the back, can be filled with gifts and chocolates. The angels' heads are made from plain fabric stuffed with cotton balls, and their faces have been drawn on with felt-tip pen.

ABOVE: Simple felt bags, big enough to contain chocolate truffles or a luxurious bar of soap, are a good way to include house guests in the festivities.
OPPOSITE: In some families, all the presents, big and small, are delivered by Santa Claus, so a sack rather than a stocking is left at the end of the bed.

make sure your **children leave a drink** for **Santa Claus** and a few carrots for his reindeer

Scouring stores and markets for beautiful and unusual Christmas decorations is a real seasonal treat, but don't forget that making your own from scratch can be just as much fun. If you have children, homemade decorations are an excellent way to keep them occupied close to Christmas. It doesn't take much to please young children already giddy with excitement at the thought of Santa Claus—just a messy afternoon making bright paperchains or baking gingerbread cookies for the tree.

homemade decorations

Making decorations with your children, whatever their ages, has to be one of the nicest ways to spend time together—the undiluted glee with which they'll throw themselves into cutting, glueing, and baking will no doubt bring back the excitement of your own childhood Christmases. Many children will have helped decorate their classrooms at school, so getting to work on their own homes will be an exciting prospect. But you may find they have rather fixed ideas about what constitutes a correctly decorated room— usually it's a wild riot of tinsel—so if that suits you, then let them go for it.

However, you may find that this is not the effect you are aiming for all over the house. Simple tree decorations made from pinecones glued together and suspended with ribbon are a good compromise—stylish enough for adult tastes, but easy enough for children to make. Slightly more complex, but just as charming, are little clothespeg fairies, snowmen, and Santa Clauses. Old-fashioned wooden clothespegs are still available from craft shops and some hardware stores. Buy a couple of packs, as clothespeg people are fun to make, and once you and your children get the hang of them, one or two fairies will not be enough. You'll want to create nativity scenes, choirs of angels, and multiple Santa Clauses.

THIS PICTURE: To create these undeniably cute snowmen, buy pompom kits and lots of wool (white for snowmen and bright red for jolly Santa Clauses) and put your children to work!
ABOVE RIGHT: Clothespeg angels, fairies, and Santas make excellent tree decorations.
BELOW RIGHT: These nativity animals are crafted from old corks. Use spent matchsticks for their spindly legs, and cut a small groove at one end of the cork, then slide in the heads, which have been drawn on to stiff card stock and cut out. Stick names on the bodies and you can use them as place-card holders for the Christmas table.

encourage your children to get creative and make their own decorations—it can be messy!

Although incredibly simple to make, felt shapes such as trees, stars, and Christmas stockings have a real homespun charm and look great on the tree. Younger children can glue the shapes together and decorate with glitter glue, while older children can sew around the edges with jolly, contrasting thread. Pompom snowmen have an irresistably kitsch appeal, and making pompoms is one of those wonderful jobs that keep children quiet for hours. Most craft stores sell pompom kits as well as wool in a variety of shades, so all you need do is set your children to work making fluffy balls in different sizes. When finished, glue three pompoms of descending size together to form little snowmen, and dress them with felt accessories. If you're a keen knitter, tiny scarves and bobble hats provide a cute finishing touch.

Bedroom windows are the ideal place for children to express their Christmas-fueled creativity, and flurries of ethereal tissue-paper snowflakes are the perfect decoration. Just cut several sheets of white tissue paper into

OPPOSITE ABOVE: A chain of paper lanterns is simple to make and looks particularly effective as part of an all-white theme. Take a piece of white paper, fold in half from top to bottom, and make regular cuts from the fold out, stopping about an inch from the edge. Open out the paper, then

Scotchtape the two shortest sides together to create a barrel, as shown. Glue on paper loops to hang the lanterns from. OPPOSITE BELOW: Popsicle sticks covered with glitter make a shimmering window display. THIS PAGE: Paper snowflakes require nimble scissorwork but look enchanting on the tree.

squares. Fold each one in half to create a triangle, then repeat to create another, smaller triangle. With the long edge at the bottom, fold the left edge in to the midline, then fold the right edge in the same way to create a tall narrow triangle with two tails, which should be cut off. Finally, get to work with scissors and snip away at the triangle's sides. Carefully open out the tissue paper to reveal a beautiful snowflake.

Glittery stars are a nice alternative to snowflakes and can be made from popsicle sticks glued together in sets of three to create six-pointed stars. First paint the popsicle sticks gold or silver, then coat them with glue and sprinkle with glitter.

Children always jump at the chance of making a mess in the kitchen, so tree decorations such as gingerbread snowmen (see page 117) and jeweled cookie stars are always hugely popular. Look out for Christmas-themed cookie cutters in kitchenware stores and catalogs. And as these decorations taste as good as they look, make several batches, because they rarely last long on the tree!

OPPOSITE: Felt decorations are easy to make—it's just a matter of snipping, glueing, and simple stitching.
ABOVE: Paper stars look stunning on the tree. Take a rectangular sheet of paper and pleat carefully. Fold in half and secure at the center with a twist of fuse wire. Cut the edges of the pleats to create pointed ends. Fan out to reveal a star and secure the ends with tape.
RIGHT: Making clothespeg people is curiously addictive! Try angels, fairies, and snowmen as well as jolly Santa Clauses.

The simplest gift becomes a luxurious treat when it's been carefully wrapped. Whatever the present, take the time to make it look good. Wrapping up a present in beautiful paper, complete with pretty ribbons and a homemade label is neither difficult nor expensive; it just requires a little thought and preparation.

gifts and gift wrapping

Although the choice of Christmas cards available in the stores improves year after year, making your own Christmas cards is incredibly satisfying and much more fun. It's also guaranteed to impress friends and family alike!

homemade cards

ABOVE: Children really enjoy printing and glueing, and making simple Christmas cards is an excellent way to let them have a go at both activities. It will also keep them occupied for some time, and although messy, you can comfort yourself with the knowledge that their work does have a purpose! Here, bold potato prints of a Christmas tree and a holly leaf have been carefully decorated with a scattering of sparkling glitter and silver stars.

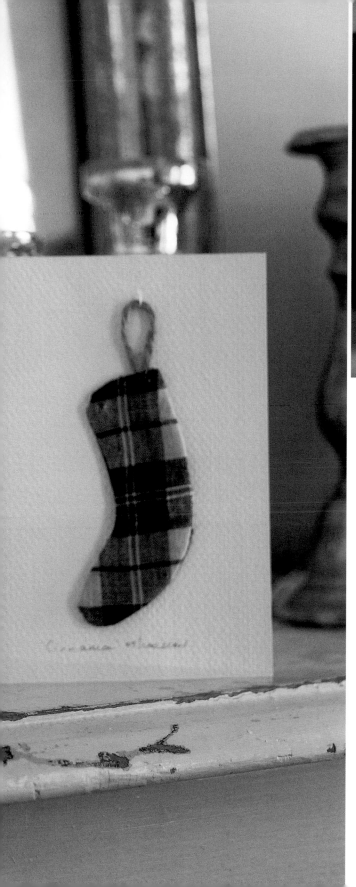

LEFT: Scraps of pretty fabric were the starting point for these simple but effective cards. The fabric was cut into the shape of a Christmas stocking and glued to high quality, heavy-weight card stock.
ABOVE: Origami paper, while not overtly Christmassy, looks very decorative when snipped into bold Christmas shapes and stuck onto contrastingly colored card stock or posterboard.

Homemade cards don't need to be complicated to be effective and, if you have children, it's exactly the kind of rainy-day project they love. Making cards is also a great way to use up those candy wrappers and scraps of fabric that we all seem to accumulate for no particular reason.

For really young children, stencils and potato prints are perfect. A simple holly leaf or Christmas tree can be quickly and easily jazzed up with glue and a sprinkling of glitter. Small children enjoy the mess that goes with painting and sticking, and most will have had some experience at nursery school.

More complex collages will keep older children occupied for hours. Seasonally shaped cookie cutters make good templates for angels, stars, and trees, and these forms can then be decorated with whatever materials you have at hand. Build snowmen from crumpled tissue paper, shredded paper towels, or cotton balls. Triangles of green crêpe paper make graphic

Christmas trees, which can then be adorned with tiny baubles and tinsel, crafted from shiny candy wrappers and rolled-up kitchen foil. Scraps of fabric and even decorative oriental origami paper can be cut into a variety of Christmassy shapes, such as stockings, crowns, and presents, and glued onto brightly colored card stock or posterboard.

Creating Christmas cards with particular friends in mind is fun as you can include jokes and references that they will really appreciate. A search through an old pile of photographs is a good starting point and will usually provide a haul of photos that didn't make the album and that you won't miss. Look for people in interesting positions or looking surprised—they can become Kings following the star, singing angels, or shepherds gazing in awe at the nativity scene. Use fabric and old wrapping paper to give your characters costumes, and the all-important star can be created with glitter, silver foil, or gold pen.

A bold, silhouetted 3-D card is an effective way to satisfy your creative urges. Take a sheet of strong white card stock and score lines so you can fold it into three. Back the middle panel with a piece of brightly colored paper (dark red or green look particularly effective) and then, using a craft knife, cut away an Alpine scene of tiny log cabins, fir trees, and snowy peaks, so they stand out against the bold backing color. The result is an enchanting minature wonderland.

ABOVE: Invest in lots of felt at the start of December. It's cheap and easy to work with, and can be used for so many Christmas projects, such as these cards. One features a collage of Santa Claus, and the other, a star embroidered with bright thread.

for really **young children**, stencils and potato prints are perfect. A simple **holly leaf** or Christmas tree can be jazzed up with **glue and glitter**

RIGHT: Give the traditional approach to wrapping a bottle of wine a twist, by trimming the wrapping with strips of paper in a contrasting color. Use a length of the contrasting paper in place of ribbon, and add a Christmas decoration as a final touch.

OPPOSITE: Beautiful wrapping doesn't require expensive materials, just a few clever tricks. Here, tissue paper in different shades of pink has been layered so that once wrapped around the package, the papers can be folded back to reveal contrasting bands of color. Trimmings have been twisted into tissue roses.
ABOVE: Make gift tokens more intriguing by presenting them in handmade envelopes. Use an ordinary envelope as your template and draw around it onto the prettiest paper you can find.

Wrapping presents on Christmas Eve is one of the nicest rituals of the season. For some reason, fiddling with ribbons, tissue paper, and tape just before the big day is much more fun than doing it piecemeal as and when the presents are bought.

gift wrapping

Obviously the bulk of presents will need to be wrapped in advance, but save some to the last minute and savor the excitement! You will, of course, need to consider how to wrap your presents much earlier than Christmas Eve, and it's a good idea to decide on a theme for all your gifts, however big or small.

Take your cue for the color and style of your wrapping from your Christmas tree. Presents wrapped in glossy red or green paper with contrasting ribbons will look magnificent piled at the foot of a traditionally dressed tree, covered with antique decorations and glass baubles. A white and gold tree would look best with lavishly wrapped presents, perhaps tied with layered organza, silk, and velvet ribbons. A Shaker-style tree adorned with pinecones and homemade gingerbread decorations calls for a similarly understated wrapping style. When it comes to stocking stuffers, there is only one option—tissue paper. Don't worry about the color—it's the crunchy, crinkly sound it makes that matters. And bear in mind that the speed at which stocking presents are unwrapped makes fancy frills a waste of time.

OPPOSITE: Little packages wrapped in simple white tissue paper
look fabulous when placed on plates and dressed with garlands of
stars and delicate glass balls.

LEFT: If you are planning to give party favors, buying boxes will be
expensive. Instead, make your own, using a store-bought box as a
template. To create the template, open the box out carefully and
draw around it on a piece of paper. Cut out the template and place
it on a piece of card stock of your choice. Draw around the
template, then cut out the box before reassembling it and finishing
with glue. Corrugated card gift boxes and velvet ribbon combine
well for a particularly sophisticated effect.

Not all presents call for straightforward wrapping; some
are awkwardly shaped and others too small or delicate. As
well as offering extra protection, a box is a great way to
ensure that a gift's shape doesn't reveal its contents,
prolonging the anticipation. You can either buy ready-made
boxes or save old packaging throughout the year to
customize with wrapping paper and ribbons in whatever
colors you are using for the rest of your presents. Gift bags,
too, are good for odd-shaped presents. Buy plain white or
colored bags to jazz up with cut-out stars, snowflakes, or
holly leaves. For something more elaborate, create a collage,
such as a Christmas tree, using papers in different textures,
weights, and colors. Matching tags can be made with
whatever you have left over, or you could incorporate a
friend's name into the design. Fabric bags are a satisfying
way to use up any odd pieces of fabric or felt that you might
have lying around. The bags can be sealed quite simply with
a length of ribbon tied in a bow.

Another way to disguise a gift's shape is to wrap it in the
shape of a large tube, with the ends secured with ribbon (like
a Christmas cracker). This is not difficult, and it is guaranteed

to create an impression. First, make a tube, using a piece of card stock (an old toilet roll is ideal for small presents), and place the present inside. Then, take a sheet of gift wrap and fold it to create pleats at regular intervals—this is important, as it ensures a full "cuff" at either end of the tube. Place the paper on a flat surface, right side down, and hold the pleats in place with a strip of Scotch tape stuck along its center. Now place the tube containing the present parallel to the pleats and centered at one end of the paper. Roll the tube along the paper until you reach the end, and seal with tape. Finally, tie with ribbon at either end. Less structured-looking wrappings can be made using tissue paper, which is easier to handle, but is also prone to tearing, so only use it on soft presents, such as gloves or socks.

Gift tokens are always a successful gift when you're feeling uninspired, but a little white envelope looks so meager next to a stack of promising presents. It's a shame,

when it comes to **stocking** stuffers, **tissue** paper makes a wonderfully **crinkly** sound

and totally unnecessary. If you are giving someone a token, a check, theater tickets, or just a crisp new $20 bill, it's worth making an effort to dress up the gift. Either buy a colorful envelope and decorate it with paper cut-outs, sequins, feathers, metallic pens, and glitter, or make your own decorative envelopes from pretty pieces of gift wrap. Use an ordinary envelope of the correct size as a template. Open it out carefully, using a paper knife if necessary, and taking care not to tear the sides. Place the opened-out envelope on the back of the paper you want to use, then draw around it with a pencil, cut it out, fold it in the right places, and glue it together. Finish off by attaching a bead to the end of a length of silver thread or fine wire, and wind it around the envelope to seal it.

And finally, should the unimaginable happen, and you realize, late on Christmas Eve, that you've completely exhausted your supplies of gift wrap, there is a solution, and it's both easy and elegant—newspaper. Newspaper has just enough stiffness and body to fold neatly, and it makes excellent replacement wrapping paper. A neat stack of presents all wrapped in newsprint and dressed with bright ribbon looks quirky and stylish, so much so that everyone will assume it's what you'd planned all along.

OPPOSITE ABOVE: Wrapping a gift in a tube is a good way to disguise its shape and also strikes the right note of fun and festivity. For instructions on how to wrap a gift in a tube, see page 108.

OPPOSITE BELOW LEFT: Personalize plain, store-bought gift bags with seasonal collages, such as these robins made from lightweight corrugated card stock and boldly colored paper.

OPPOSITE BELOW RIGHT AND LEFT: What could be better than an edible label on your present? Decorate gingerbread hearts (see the recipe on page 117) with names piped in white frosting, then tie to gifts with jaunty gingham bows.

Christmas is a sociable time, and it's always nice to take a thank you gift for friends giving parties. Chocolates or a bottle of wine are the obvious things to fall back on, but a homemade present is always appreciated far more. These days we are all so time-poor that the thought of a friend not just taking the time to think about your present but spending time making it, is incredibly touching.

homemade gifts

Don't make the mistake of thinking that giving homemade gifts means you will have to spend most of December chained to a sewing machine. Keep things simple: a posy of winter flowers and foliage from the garden, tied with a length of thick velvet ribbon, is a beautiful alternative to a store-bought bunch of flowers. Likewise, homemade tree decorations, such as a trio of dainty clothespeg fairies or winged angels nestled in a pretty box, is a much more personal gift, and can be added to the tree immediately.

For someone cooking Christmas dinner for a large number of people, table decorations such as angelic place card holders (see page 70) or cardamom pears (see page 71) would be perfect. Easier still, you could buy lots of fat church candles, wrap a sheet of beeswax around each one, and use thick velvet ribbon to bundle them in threes, secured with a simple bow.

Making a spicy winter potpourri has all the satisfaction of cooking but with none of the mess or anxiety of recipes, measurements, and oven times. Good-quality essential oils such as sandalwood, cedarwood, and frankincense are widely available. Choose the ones you like and which best conjure up the season. Look out for unusual dried ingredients for the potpourri itself; most good florists have a selection of fir cones and dried spices such as star anise and cinnamon sticks, as well as foliage and fruit.

In places where a cold Christmas is the norm, a snuggly hot-water bottle complete with cover makes a great present—it's perfect for warming a cold bed and is the sort of little luxury people rarely buy for themselves. Although good fake fur is expensive, the small quantity needed here makes it affordable. Use the hot water bottle to make a template, then buy enough fabric to make a couple of covers (as no doubt you'll want one, too!). Choose a contrasting lining, such as bright pink silk, and a length of ribbon to match.

OPPOSITE ABOVE: Candles are always gratefully received, especially at Christmastime.

OPPOSITE BELOW: Christmas decorations make great thank you presents in lieu of the more usual box of chocolates or bottle of wine.

THIS PAGE: Make up a large batch of Christmas-scented potpourri, and bag it up for friends and family. A simple homemade label tied on with pretty ribbon is all that it needs in the way of wrapping.

Place your fabric right sides together and stitch around the sides, leaving the top open. Hem the top opening, pop your hot water bottle inside, and use the ribbon to tie the cover around the neck of the bottle. Two belt-loops to hold the ribbon in place would be a useful finishing touch.

Photograph albums are always useful presents and make great Christmas gifts for couples who've just gotten married or have had their first child—two events that seem to trigger a storm of photographs. To elevate your gift above the albums they'll doubtless have, take an ordinary album with good-quality plain pages and cover it with a piece of fabric.

Notebooks and diaries can be customized in just the same way. For a high-school graduate just off to college, a diary

made from a plain hard-backed notebook covered with fabric such as ticking or chintz (depending on his or her tastes, of course), or a collage of photos of friends and family, would make a particularly thoughtful present. For both these ideas, it's worth visiting the sale sections of smart stationers, where you might find that an excellent album or notebook with a slightly shop-worn cover has been massively reduced, leaving you free to really go to town with the new cover.

Edible presents always go down well at Christmas. After all, this is the time of year when everyone is in the mood for a little indulgence. But, tempting though it is to hotfoot it to the nearest fancy delicatessen in search of expensive oils and wine, this is a wonderful opportunity to make something instead. Homemade cookies or gingerbread tree decorations are a far less predictable and more thoughtful present than a box of chocolates.

edible gifts

Gingerbread cookies are perfect gifts for children, especially when they're decorated with personalized frosting.

gingerbread

Sift the flour, baking powder, salt, and spices into a bowl.

Melt the butter in a saucepan and add the sugars. Let cool, then add eggs.

Gradually combine butter mixture and flour. The mixture will be very sticky, so transfer it to a bowl, cover with plastic wrap, and put in the refrigerator overnight, or until firm enough to handle easily.

Roll out dough to a quarter-inch (5 mm) thick and cut into preferred shapes. For tree decorations and tags, make a hole at the top with a chopstick. Bake in a preheated oven at 350°F (180°C, gas 4) for 10 minutes.

Turn out onto wire racks to cool, then decorate with royal frosting.

Royal frosting
Beat the sugar and egg white together until smooth. If using several colors, divide the mixture into different bowls and add food coloring. Fill pastry bags and decorate.

2¹/₂ cups (340 g) all-purpose flour

1 teaspoon baking powder

1 teaspoon salt

1 teaspoon nutmeg

2 teaspoons cinnamon

2 teaspoons ground ginger

2 sticks (225 g) butter

1 cup (225 g) caster sugar

³/₄ cup (170 g) soft dark brown sugar

2 eggs, beaten

ROYAL FROSTING

1 egg white

1 cup (150 g) confectioners' sugar

Food coloring, as you wish

Cookie cutters

Greased cookie sheet

Pastry bag with plain nozzle

MAKES 15 COOKIES

Once you've tasted these, you'll never eat a store-bought marshmallow again. Great for toasting over the fire.

marshmallows

1 cup of cold
water (250 ml)

3 tablespoons
granulated
gelatin

3¼ cups (675 g)
granulated sugar

1⅓ cups (425 g)
golden syrup

1 teaspoon salt

2 teaspoons
vanilla extract

Greased baking
tray, 9" x 12" (22 x
30 cm)

Confectioners'
sugar, for dusting

*MAKES ABOUT 30
MARSHMALLOWS*

Pour three-quarters of the water into a
stand mixer and sprinkle with the gelatin.
Let soften.

Put the rest of the water in a saucepan, add
the granulated sugar, golden syrup, salt, and
vanilla extract, and bring to boil until a
sugar thermometer reads 240°F (116°C) or
the mixture reaches the soft-ball stage.

In the stand mixer, start whisking the
gelatin mixture on a low speed and slowly
pour the hot syrup down the side of the
bowl. Gradually increase the speed to high,
then leave it on high until the mixture is
white and cool, and stiff peaks have
formed. This could take 30 minutes.

Pour into the baking tray. Cover with plastic
wrap and leave overnight. Turn out onto a
surface covered in confectioners' sugar, and
cut into squares with an oiled, sharp knife.

*Children adore these, and will happily help in both the
making and the eating of them. They look great on a white-
frosted Christmas cake, too—kitsch yet charming.*

sugar snowmen

2½ cups (500 g)
confectioners'
sugar, sifted

1 large egg white,
beaten

1 tablespoon
golden syrup or
corn syrup

Pink and green
food coloring

Silver balls and
other decorations,
as you wish

*MAKES 10
SNOWMEN*

Put a cup of the confectioners' sugar in a
bowl along with the egg white and beat
with a wooden spoon until smooth.

Add the syrup and a half-cup of the
remaining sugar. Beat until smooth.

Add the rest of the sugar, except for a
handful to sprinkle on the countertop. If
the mixture becomes difficult to work at
this point, add a tiny bit of water.

Divide the sugar dough into three balls.
Add a couple of drops of pink coloring to
one, and green to another. Cover the sugar
dough with plastic wrap while not using.

Take a lump and knead it on the sugared
counter. Form the round body first, then
the scarf, and then the head. Vary the hat
designs. Use silver balls or other decorations
to make buttons, eyes, and noses.

Let harden for a couple of days in a dry,
cool place.

These look just as good as they taste and are the perfect present for real gourmets. If you are going to a number of parties this Christmas, make up several batches which you can box up and give to your hosts.

crystallized chestnuts

1 pound (450 g)
fresh chestnuts

2¹⁄₃ cups (450 g)
granulated sugar

²⁄₃ cup (150 ml)
water

1 teaspoon
vanilla extract

MAKES 1¹⁄₂
POUNDS (675 g)
OF CHESTNUTS

Pierce the stiff skin of the chestnuts with a sharp knife and then boil for 20 minutes. Peel while still warm.

Put the sugar and water in a saucepan and dissolve over low heat to make a syrup. Work slowly, making sure you don't leave any sugar on the sides of the pan, then boil for one minute.

Add the chestnuts and the vanilla extract and boil for another 10 minutes.

Remove chestnuts and drain on a wire rack. Set the syrup aside and cover it.

Let the chestnuts sit for 24 hours, then re-boil the syrup, add the chestnuts, and simmer for 10 minutes or until coated.

Drain and let cool before transfering to a gift box or jar.

With their yummy combination of fruit, nuts, and chocolate, these make ideal Christmas cookies.

florentines

¹⁄₂ stick (55 g)
butter

¹⁄₄ cup (55 g)
sugar

2 teaspoons
honey

A heaped ¹⁄₃ cup
(55 g) all-purpose
flour

1¹⁄₄ cups (150 g)
mixture of
candied cherries,
citrons, or candied
peel, blanched
and chopped
almonds

One 7-oz (200 g)
dark chocolate
bar, melted

2 cookie sheets,
lined with
parchment paper

MAKES 20
COOKIES

Melt the butter, sugar, and honey in a heavy saucepan. Remove from the heat and add the flour, citrons, cherries, and almonds. Mix to a smooth paste.

Drop teaspoons of the mixture onto the paper-lined cookie sheets, leaving space for expansion, and flatten them with a spoon.

Bake in a preheated oven at 350°F (180°C, gas 4) for 8 to 10 minutes or until golden. Remove from oven, let sit for a couple of minutes, and then transfer to a wire rack.

When cool, you can make the florentines perfectly round with a sharp knife, or leave them as they are. Paint the underside with the melted chocolate. Just before the chocolate hardens, make wavy marks with a fork. Let set until the chocolate is completely hard.

Flavored oils are always appreciated. They look lovely and are easy to make. Search for attractive glass bottles in department stores and specialty kitchen shops.

olive oil

Enough good-quality extra-virgin olive oil to fill your chosen bottles.

A selection of the following: sprigs of rosemary and thyme, peppercorns, dried chiles, bay leaves.

Place any of the dried herbs and spices into your bottle, and then top up with oil.

Make a decorative label by writing on a pretty tag and securing a Christmas decoration around the neck of the bottle.

Sloe gin looks stunning and is so delicious that, once open, a bottle rarely lasts long. Sloes can be hard to find, so if necessary, substitute an equal number of blueberries.

sloe gin

Good-quality gin

Approx. 1lb (450 g) sloes

1 cup (225 g) sugar

2–3 drops of almond extract (optional)

Large bottle or jar or two smaller bottles to hold 1 liter of liquid if using above quantities.

In early autumn, gather as many sloes as you can, weigh them, and then prick each one with a needle.

Fill your bottle to the half-way mark with the fruit, then add the sugar.

Fill up the rest of the bottle with gin (and almond extract, if using).

Ideally let the mixture sit for three to six months, then strain and re-bottle the clear ruby-colored liquor and let it sit another three to six months. You can speed up the process by regularly shaking the bottle, but this may impair the depth of flavor.

sources

ALASKA CHRISTMAS STORE
P. O. Box 727
Skagway, AK 99840
800-770-5770
www.alaskachristmasstore.com
*In addition to selling a wide
selection of ornaments and
collectibles, they specialize in
Alaskan-themed Nativities, angels,
and Santa decorations.*

ALWAYS CHRISTMAS
3033 West Parker
Plano, TX 75023
877-596-7695
www.alwayschristmastexas.com
*North Texas' largest year-round
Christmas store carries ornaments
and decorations, as well as trees,
lights, and collectibles.*

BED BATH & BEYOND
Locations nationwide
Call 800-462-3966 or visit
www.bedbathandbeyond.com for
details of your nearest store
*Candles, tableware, decorations,
and novelty items for the holidays.*

BLOOMINGDALE'S
Locations nationwide
Visit www.bloomingdales.com for
details of your nearest store
*A selection of gifts and decorations
for the holidays.*

**BRONNER'S CHRISTMAS
WONDERLAND**
25 Christmas Lane, P. O. Box 176
Frankenmuth, MI 48734-0176
989-652-9931
www.bronners.com
*Over 50,000 gifts and 400 Nativity
scenes are available.*

CARLTON CARDS
Locations nationwide
Call 800-679-8343 or visit
www.carltoncards.com for details
of your nearest store
*Cards, ornaments, decorations,
collectibles, heirloom ornaments,
and more for the holidays.*

CHRISTMASCRACKERS.COM
www.christmas-crackers-usa.com
*This online distributor offers a wide
variety of decorative party crackers
designs, as well as all the necessary
cracker components if you want to
make your own.*

THE CHRISTMAS SHOP
307 Bull Street
Savannah, GA 31404
800-569-0330
www.the-christmas-shop.com
*Hard-to-find Christmas and
seasonal ornaments, decorations,
and collectibles.*

THE CHRISTMAS SHOP
424 Duke of Gloucester Street
Williamsburg, VA 23185
757-229-2514
www.christmasshopwilliamsburg.
com
*The widest selection of
Williamsburg-themed ornaments
available, as well as many
collectible lines.*

CHRISTMAS SPIRIT SHOP
80 Main Street
Bar Harbor, ME 04609
800-242-2913
www.christmasspiritshop.com
*This store offers dozens of
personalized Christmas ornaments,
as well as Christmas books, Santas,
Nativities, and Christmas music.*

**CHRISTMAS TREES, WREATHS,
AND DECORATIONS**
P. O. Box 28
Culver, IN 46511
800-458-0445
www.christmas-trees-wreaths-
decorations.com
*Natural and artificial Christmas
trees, wreaths, lights, garlands, and
topiaries.*

COST PLUS WORLD MARKET
Locations nationwide
Visit www.costplus.com for details
of your nearest store
*A specialty retailer that carries an
extensive selection of tableware,
ornaments, food, decorations, gifts,
Christmas crackers, and papers
from around the world.*

CRATE AND BARREL
Locations nationwide
Call 800-967-6696 or visit
www.crateandbarrel.com for
details of your nearest store
*Good-value, stylish tableware, table
linen, and candles.*

CREATIVE CANDLES
P. O. Box 412514
Kansas City, MO 64141
816-474-9711
www.creativecandles.com
*Hand-dipped, state-of-the-art
tapers, pillars, and spheres in 44
designer colors.*

FLAX ART & DESIGN
1699 Market Street
San Francisco, CA 94103
415-552-2355
www.flaxart.com
*Creative candles, ribbons,
ornaments, gifts, and an enormous
selection of art supplies.*

FRANK'S NURSERY
Locations nationwide
Visit www.franks.com for details
of your nearest nursery.
*Frank's is a reliable source for
Christmas trees, wreaths, flowers,
and craft supplies.*

HALLMARK
Locations nationwide
Visit www.hallmark.com for
details of your nearest store
*Large stock of Christmas and
greeting cards, gift wrap, novelty
items, ornaments, and more.*

IKEA
Locations nationwide
Visit www.ikea-usa.com for details
of your nearest store
*Contemporary Swedish Christmas
decorations and food in season.*

ILLUMINATIONS
Locations nationwide
Call 800-621-2998 or visit
www.illuminations.com for details
of your nearest store
*Candles and accessories, tabletop
decorations, mirrors, accent
furniture, crystal, and more. All
candles are made from refined
waxes that are classified as food-
grade materials.*

JAM PAPER
111 Third Avenue
New York, NY 10003
Call 212-473-6666 or visit
www.jampaper.com for details
of their other two stores
*Suppliers of specialty papers,
ribbons, envelopes, and packaging.
Three stores in New York and New
Jersey, as well as an extensive mail-
order and online catalogue service.*

JOANN FABRICS
Locations nationwide
Visit www.joann.com for details of
your nearest store
*A superstore for fabric, craft
materials, patterns, sewing, and
holiday supplies.*

KATE'S PAPERIE
561 Broadway
New York, NY 10012
212-941-9816
Visit www.katespaperie.com for
details of their five stores
Specialty papers and stationery.

KMART
Locations nationwide
Visit www.kmart.com for details of
your nearest store
*Candles, tableware, ornaments, and
decorations.*

MACY'S
Locations nationwide
Visit www.macys.com for details
of your nearest store
*Well-known for their beautiful
Christmas displays, Macy's sells
ornaments, decorations, tableware,
wrapping paper, and festive gifts.*

MICHAELS
Locations nationwide
Visit www.michaels.com for
details of your nearest store
*A huge selection of every kind of art
and craft materials.*

OUTER BANKS CHRISTMAS SHOP
621 South US 64
Manteo, NC 27954
800-470-2838
www.outerbankschristmas.com
*Browse through room after room
(36 in all) of fine gifts, music boxes,
jewelry, toys, decoys, candles,
stationery, and more.*

PAPER ACCESS
23 West 18th Street
New York, NY 10011
800-PAPER-01
www.paperaccess.com
*Handmade and specialty paper, gift
wrap, ribbon, tags, and cards.*

PAPYRUS
Stores nationwide
Visit www.papyrusonline.com for
details of your nearest store
*Cards, paper, ribbon, gift wrap, and
custom printing.*

PEARL PAINT
Locations nationwide
Call 800-221-6845 or visit
www.pearlpaint.com for details of
your nearest store
Art and craft supplies.

PIER 1 IMPORTS
Locations nationwide
Visit www.pier1.com for details of
your nearest store
*Candles, decorations, potpourri, and
festive tableware.*

POTTERY BARN
Locations nationwide
Call 888-226-3537 or visit
www.potterybarn.com for details
of your nearest store
*Stockings, decorations, tableware,
candles, and accessories.*

RESTORATION HARDWARE
Locations nationwide
Call 800-762-1005 or visit
www.restorationhardware.com for
details of your nearest store
*Ornaments, housewares, and
vintage-style holiday gifts.*

SAKS FIFTH AVENUE
Locations nationwide
Call 877-551-SAKS or visit

www.saksfifthavenue.com for
details of your nearest store
*Holiday gifts and decorations, and
the famed window displays in New
York City's Rockefeller Center location.*

SIMPLY LUMINARIES
www.simplyluminaries.com
*Everything you need to create safe
holiday luminaries, as well as pre-
made crystal luminaries.*

SMITH & HAWKEN
Locations nationwide
Call 800-940-1170 or visit
www.smithandhawken.com for
details of your nearest store
*High-quality products including
flowers, wreaths, and boughs.*

SPECIALTIES IN WOOL
P. O. Box 100
Worcester, VT 05682
800-242-9427
www.specialtiesinwool.com
*Vermont-made woolen stockings,
ornaments, and tree skirts.*

TARGET
Locations nationwide
Visit www.target.com for details
of your nearest store
Ornaments and decorations.

**THE UNION SQUARE HOLIDAY
MARKET**
14th Street between Broadway
and University Place
New York, NY
*Each year, New York City's Union
Square features a Holiday Bazaar.
A great place to find handmade
goods, toys, crafts, and ornaments.*

WESTERN SILVER
www.westernsilver.com
*Silver Christmas ornaments, gifts,
flatware, and accessories.*

WILLIAMS-SONOMA
Locations nationwide
Visit www.williams-sonoma.com
for details of your nearest store
*This housewares retailer has plenty
to offer the holiday table, from
gingerbread cookie mix to pans for
roasting the holiday bird.*

business
credits

**VIVIEN LAWRENCE
INTERIOR DESIGN**
+44 20 8209 0058/0562
www.vlinteriordesign.com
Pages 36–37, 50, 51c & r, 66

EMILY MEDLEY
Designer
emilymedley@mac.com
Page 1, 54, 59, 87, 88–89, 90r,
92–93, 96-97

CLARE NASH
House Stylist
+44 20 8742 9991
Pages 28-31, 59, 82-83

CLEMENTINE YOUNG
Cook and food writer
07799 628276
clementineyoung@hotmail.com
Page 18l, 43c, 116, 118-121

THE SWEDISH CHAIR
48 Heathhurst Road
Sanderstead
Surrey CR2 OBA
England
+44 20 8657 8560
www.theswedishchair.com
Painter David Sandström, Sweden
+ 46 90 98049
Pages 16-21, 42, 72, 82, 91, 106r

picture credits

All photography by Jo Tyler.
Key: a=above, b=below, r=right, l=left, c=center

1 Clothespeg angels made by Emily Medley; 2 Painted decorations by Emily Readett-Bayley; 4 Basket of baubles from Dawn Gren; 6 Knitted toy from Baileys Home & Garden, dogs on "Shetland Plaid" fabric in cinnamon from Mulberry Home, tartan cushion from Anta; 7 Art Director Hans Blomquist's home in London; 8–9 Owner of Adamczewski, Hélène Adamczewski's house in Lewes/All china, linen, & glass from Adamczewski; 10l Silk flower from VV Rouleaux, bird from New Covent Garden Market; 11 Black baubles from DZD, silk flowers from VV Rouleaux, ribbon from New Covent Garden Market, antique fabric hearts and slippers from Tobias & The Angel, wrapping paper from Paperchase; 12 Candles from Ethos Candles, glasses & glass cake stands from The Dining Room Shop, crackers from Napier Industries; 13 Glass bead berry garland from VV Rouleaux; 14l Tartan "Shetland Plaid" from Mulberry Home; 15r pressed-glass cake stands all from The Dining Room Shop; 16–21 Owner of The Swedish Chair, Lena Renkel Eriksson's house in London; 16 Furniture from The Swedish Chair, china, table linen, flower vases/bowls, hanging decorations, little men, & checked table linen all from The Blue Door; 17l Red wooden decoration from The Blue Door; 17ar Tree decorations from The Blue Door; 17br Napkins, china plate & straw decorations from The Blue Door; 18l Gingerbread house by Clementine Young; 20 Nordic garland from Dawn Gren; 20–21l straw hanging from The Blue Door; 21c–21r Advent candle & dish from The Blue Door; 22–27 Abigail Ahern's home in London; 22r–23l Glass baubles from The Christmas Shop; 24 Bead garlands from VV Rouleaux, straw decorations from Baileys Home & Garden; 25 Taper candles from Ethos Candles; 27l Icicle lights from Woolworths; 27r Snowflake decorations from Paperchase; 28–31 House Stylist Clare Nash's home in London; 28r Striped baubles from Paperchase; 29 Sculpture armature wire made by Alec Tiranti; 30 Baubles from Paperchase, sparkly sticks from New Covent Garden Market; 31r–33 Clare and Alex's home in London; 32 Paper lanterns by Angel Works; 34–35 Bears and bead trees from Paperchase; 36–37 A family home in London, interior design by Vivien Lawrence; 36l Butterflies from VV Rouleaux, shells from New Covent Garden Market; 36r–37l Silk flowers from VV Rouleaux and Flowers by Novelty, papers from Paperchase; 37r Butterflies from VV Rouleaux; 38a Fabric slippers and hearts made from antique fabrics from Tobias & The Angel; 38b Glass baubles from New Covent Garden Market; 39 Beaded flowers from VV Rouleaux, bird from New Covent Garden Market; 40–41 Owner of Adamczewski, Hélène Adamczewski's house in Lewes; 40 Pinecones from New Covent Garden Market, wood-look paper from Paperchase; 41al Cinnamon sticks from New Covent Garden Market; 41bl Knitted toy from Baileys Home & Garden, bronze baubles from DZD; 42 Owner of The Swedish Chair, Lena Renkel Eriksson's house in London; 42l White sticks from New Covent Garden Market; 42r–43l Striped ribbon from VV Rouleaux, wooden teddy decorations and tree decorations from Paperchase, tin heart decorations from Grace & Favour; 43c Biscuits by Clementine Young; 43r Engraved bauble and crochet snowflake from Habitat; 44 Sculpture armature wire made by Alec Tiranti, thin stripe baubles and small baubles from Paperchase, thick stripe baubles from Habitat; 45 White sticks from New Covent Garden Market, clear iridescent baubles from The Christmas Shop; 46 Crackle baubles from New Covent Garden Market; 47ar Apple decorations from New Covent Garden Market; 47b Nut garland from Grace & Favour; 49r Jo Tyler; 50, 51c & r A family home in London, interior design by Vivien Lawrence; 50 Butterflies and beaded garland from VV Rouleaux; 51l Jo Tyler; 51c–51r Beaded wreath from VV Rouleaux; 52 Art Director Hans Blomquist's home in London; 52l Twig heart wreath from Grace & Favour; 52r Dried oranges and fruit slices from New Covent Garden Market; 53 Owner of Adamczewski, Hélène Adamczewski's house in Lewes/ Peppercorns from New Covent Garden Market; 54 Bedspread made by Emily Medley, paper Santa Claus garland from VV Rouleaux; 55b Owner of Adamczewski, Hélène Adamczewski's house in Lewes/Twig wreath from Paperchase; 55r Slipper and heart decorations from Tobias & The Angel; 56 Cards from Paperchase; 57 Snowflake decorations from DZD; 58 Mini baubles and cards from Paperchase; 59 House Stylist Clare Nash's home in London/Felt cards made by Emily Medley, cut glass drops from Paperchase; 62b Jo Tyler; 62–63 Sally Butler and Tom Carter's house in London; 62ar Gingham ribbon from Temptation Alley; 62b White ceramic decorations from Habitat; 63c Painted wooden decorations by Emily Readett-Bayley; 64l Mitten garland from Baileys Home & Garden; 64br Wooden dove from Grace & Favour; 64r–65 Art Director Hans Blomquist's home in London/fabric decorations by Caroline Zoob, etched glass baubles from The Pier; 66 A family home in London, interior design by Vivien Lawrence; 66–67 Owner of Adamczewski, Hélène Adamczewski's house in Lewes/Wooden stars from Paperchase, scarves from Ford Barton; 68–69 Jo Tyler/ "Shetland Plaid" from Mulberry Home Collection, crackers from Napier Industries; 69r Sheep from Ford Barton; 70–71 Owner of Adamczewski, Hélène Adamczewski's house in Lewes; 71 China, glass, & linen from Adamczewski; 72 Owner of The Swedish Chair, Lena Renkel Eriksson's house in London; 72l Linen and bowl from The Blue Door; 72r Linen and plate from The Blue Door; 73 Sally Butler and Tom Carter's house in London/Cake stand from Grace & Favour, beeswax sheets from The Hive; 74–75 Clare and Alex's home in London; 74ar Ribbon from Temptation Alley; 74br Sweets from Selfridges; 75 Robin from New Covent Garden Market, white Christmas tree from DZD, candles, paper cups, plates & tissue paper from Paperchase; 76–77 Beeswax sheet from The Hive; 78a Glass hurricane lantern from Adamczewski; 80l Beeswax candles from The Hive; 80–81 Votive candle-holders from Baileys Home & Garden; 81r Green ribbon from Temptation Alley, spangley bauble from Grace & Favour; 82 Owner of The Swedish Chair, Lena Renkel Eriksson's house in London; 82l Felt bag from Plümo; 82br Felt decorations from Plümo; 82–83 House Stylist Clare Nash's home in London/Felt from The Cloth Shop, baby socks from Trotters; 84b Tissue paper from Paperchase; 85 Little buckets from New Covent Garden Market; 86 Stocking by Caroline Zoob; 87 Clare and Alex's home in London/ Vintage fabric stockings made by Emily Medley; 88–89 Fleece fabric from Boroviks, stockings made by Emily Medley, corduroy fabric from Textile King, wrapping paper from Liberty; 89r Owner of Adamczewski, Hélène Adamczewski's house in Lewes/ Socks from Ford Barton; 90l Angels by Angel Works; 90r Felt bags made by Emily Medley; 91 Owner of The Swedish Chair, Lena Renkel Eriksson's house in London/Paper by Cath Kidston at Liberty, gingham from John Lewis, burlap from New Covent Garden Market; 92–93 Clothespeg angels and pom-pom snowman made by Emily Medley; 96–97 Felt decorations and clothespeg Santa made by Emily Medley; 98–99 Wood-look paper from Paperchase; 100–101 Stocking cards by Caroline Zoob; 101l Card & origami paper from Paperchase; 103 Snowball candle from Baileys Home & Garden; 104 Tissue paper from Paperchase; 105l Glitter paper, glass buttons, & silver thread from Liberty, glitter butterflies from Baileys Home & Garden; 106l Star garland from VV Rouleaux; 106r–107l Owner of The Swedish Chair, Lena Renkel Eriksson's house in London/Cake plate from Grace & Favour, ribbed card from Paperchase; 108l Wooden tag from Grace & Favour; 109a Gift tags from Paperchase; 109b Silk flowers from Flowers by Novelty; 110a Pear from Emily Readett-Bayley, wrapping paper from Paperchase; 110bl Plain bags from Selfridges, card from Paperchase; 111 Gingham ribbon from Temptation Alley; 112a Pillar candles from Prices Candles, beeswax sheets from The Hive; 114l Fake fur from The Cloth Shop; 114r Tartan mug and bowl from Anta, pouches and runner made from "Shetland Plaid" from Mulberry Home; 115 Photo album and ribbon from Paperchase; 116 Cookies made by Clementine Young, gingham ribbon from Temptation Alley; 118–121 Marshmallows, snowmen, crystallized chestnuts, and florentines made by Clementine Young; 123 Wooden tags from Grace & Favour.

index

Figures in italics indicate captions.

acknowledgments

Thanks should go to the following people for all their hard work and creativity: Clementine Young for all the delicious edible gifts and decorations; Emily Medley and Vicky Robinson for getting to work with felt, paper, glitter, and glue to create all the homemade decorations; Dawn Gren for her tireless help on the shoots; Clare Packer for the beautiful paper Advent calendar on page 84, and Pete Martin for supplying the magnificent Christmas trees. Huge thanks should also go to everyone who let us invade their houses, especially Amanda Vesey and Georgina Hammick, whose homes also doubled up as hotels!